Yes, Boss

by Scott Seldin

BLYTHE-PENNINGTON, LTD.

CROTON-ON-HUDSON, NEW YORK 10520

B
K71 oo
VILLE

Library of Congress Catalog Card Number: 82-72103

ISBN 0-943778-01-8

First Printing, October, 1982

Printed in the United States

Book design by Rudi Bass

Photographs printed by Lexington Labs, Inc., N.Y.C.

To the four of us

August 21, 1978. Hervé Villechaize, 3′11″, thirty-five-year old co-star of the hit TV show "Fantasy Island" is a guest on "The Merv Griffin Show." He's asked about the house he's just bought in the Los Angeles area.

"You live in that big house all by yourself?" Merv asks.

"No," Hervé answers, "I live there with my best friend, Scott, who is a writer, and his wife Sandy, who is an artist."

October 15, 1978. 8:30 a.m. A moving van backs slowly into Hervé's driveway and stops in front of forty well-taped cartons of all sizes, gathered from local supermarkets and liquor stores. Sandy and I help two young moving men itemize the contents of the cartons.

"Where you want all this stuff shipped to?" one of the movers asks.

"New York City," I tell him. "Soon as we get an address you'll be the first to know."

We show them our furniture upstairs. "All of this goes," I say, motioning toward a chest of drawers, a queen-size bed, a disassembled couch and bookcase. I sign an insurance form and we return to the driveway. The first of the cartons is carried by one of the moving men up a wooden ramp and into the empty belly of the van.

9:30 a.m. Hervé's driver, Ben, arrives in a Burbank Studios stationwagon. As he walks toward the house he takes in the four of us and the van and asks, "Where you going?"

"New York," I answer. "Things have fallen apart for us here."

"Sorry to hear that," he says. He shakes hands goodbye, wishes us luck and strolls into the house.

A few minutes later, Hervé's bodyguard, **Maribeth**, arrives in her sporty blue car. She works for James Investigation Agency and is perfect for the job with her pixie blonde hair style, even Wasp features and attractive fortyish appearance. She's a mother of six and knows this day has been brewing since we all returned from Hawaii, a few hellish weeks ago. A brief, sad hello and she enters the house.

I put an arm around Sandy's shoulder and she says, "It's hard to believe this is happening. I feel numb."

We stare blankly at the moving men as they load the van. Perhaps another twenty minutes pass before Sandy suddenly remembers a salad bowl in the kitchen which we've forgotten to pack. She walks into the house and when she returns with it, her face is ashen.

"What is it?" I ask.

She answers, "As I passed through the kitchen I saw Maribeth holding a gun. She said Hervé had just given it to her. It looked like his .38."

Visions of Hervé's .38 caliber Special dance in my head and the heads of the movers who overhear Sandy. They pick up the pace of the move and I join in, carrying cartons up the wooden ramp into the van.

10 a.m. Hervé emerges from the house the way an army general might emerge from an indecisive battle. He walks stiffly and directly toward Ben's stationwagon, passing Sandy and me without a glance or word exchanged.

He is followed out of the house by Ben, and moments later by Maribeth, who hugs us warmly with tears in her eyes. "Take care," she says.

As she walks quickly toward her car, Sandy calls after her, "You take care, too. Don't let him do to you what he did to us."

For a split second all motion stops, then continues as Hervé climbs into the back seat of the stationwagon, Ben starts the engine, and Maribeth slides behind the wheel of her car.

Hervé's ex-wife, Anne, is the last to leave the house. She

5

embraces Sandy and me goodbye, whispering in my ear before joining Hervé in the stationwagon, "I'll keep in touch."

The moving men can't take their eyes off the unfolding drama. They watch the farewells as if viewing a funeral for the living. And it is a funeral. An eight-year friendship dies a hard and sudden death as Hervé's entourage heads toward the Burbank Studios. Best friends have parted in a matter of weeks, leaving the ruins of shared memories to be interred with the passage of time.

Spring—1970

Sandy and I first meet Anne and Hervé in a small-town, New Jersey pharmacy, around the corner from the church where our mutual friend is about to be married. We recognize each other from recent stories told by our friend, the bride.

Hervé is memorably dressed in a candy-cane striped sports jacket and straw hat. His very small size and striking appearance have immediate and powerful impact.

Anne is sweet and shy and full of love. A good chemistry is generated among the four of us and within minutes we're communicating with ease and humor, spontaneity and affection.

As we talk in the pharmacy, a young man sporting a bristling moustache and wedding clothes approaches us and says, "Hi—you folks going to the wedding?"

We nod and he smiles mischievously. Lowering his voice he asks, "In honor of the occasion would you care to share a joint with me on the back steps of the church?"

His question takes us by surprise. We laugh and can't think of any reason why we shouldn't—in honor of the occasion.

We walk with him and his wife to the steps and share a skinny joint. Then, suppressing peals of laughter, we walk into the church and sit together on a long wooden bench.

The ceremony resonates with holy vows by the bride and groom kneeling on velvet pillows. We manage to contain our silliness until after the ceremony when the wedding party leaves the church for a barbeque reception in the backyard of the bride's parents' house. Over sizzling beef, champagne and potato salad, Sandy, Anne, Hervé and I discover we have much in common. Besides a shared irreverent vision of life, we're all in our twenties, recently married, and aspiring artists. Sandy is a batik painter. Anne is a painter. Hervé is a painter and more recently an actor. I'm a writer and an independent ½" videotape producer. We're all interested in photography and we're all working toward a breakthrough that will allow us to make a living as artists.

During the barbeque I listen to Hervé speak in his French-accented, slightly lisped, broken English and suddenly recall where I've seen him before. "Weren't you in a film called 'Chappaqua'?"

He looks startled. "You saw it? Not many people saw it."

"I remember it. You were on the screen for just a few seconds but I remember you."

He smiles. "The film was made by Conrad Rook. William Burroughs and Allen Ginsberg were in it."

The wedding party lasts through the afternoon and before Sandy and I leave for our apartment on Thompson Street in Manhattan, we exchange addresses and phone numbers with Hervé and Anne. The four of us sense we could become good friends.

But we lose contact until a few months later when Sandy and I spot Anne crossing Thompson Street on her way to their loft on Greene Street. We're happy to see each other and agree to meet in their loft in a few days.

During the following months we visit each other on Green Street and Thompson Street and our friendship grows. We share struggles, hopes and frustrations—drinking wine, telling stories and filling in our past histories. An unspoken trust develops among us as does affection, loyalty and support.

Anne and Hervé have been married about two years. Sandy and I are married but a few months. The seventies are also only months old; the new decade is still without shape or identity. The feeling carried over from the sixties is that all things are possible. It is a feeling the four of us share.

Anne and Hervé live in a section of Manhattan that has yet to become known as fashionable Soho. In 1970 it is a desolate area of cast-iron factory buildings, garbage-strewn side streets, and trucks which load and unload all day long. A handful of artists live surreptitiously on a few of these factory floors, drawn to the area by the large space available at low rents. Anne and Hervé are among this handful of artists. The building where they live has a freight elevator, is without heat during the weekends and at night, and has a sign on the ground floor which reads Foreplay Studios. Their spacious upper floor is divided into two sections by a large plasterboard wall they've built to separate their area from the artists with whom they share the floor.

Anne's and Hervé's loft is sparsely furnished but has definite character. They've built a large sleeping platform from wood found on the streets. Beneath this platform is a desk and closet. Most of their loft's furnishings are street finds: a living room table compliments of Con Edison which once used this same "table" to roll and store cable; two-by-fours used as bookshelves, supported by empty-lot bricks; found lamps, chairs, mirrors and magazines, all gifts of the streets.

Anne and Hervé are a unique looking couple, even for Manhattan.

Anne is about five feet, with opalescent skin and pretty features. Her moist, doe-like brown eyes and long lashes are her physical afterimage. She has a green thumb for plants, a small-town New Jersey upbringing and rebellious spirit.

She tells the story of how she met Hervé while they were

attending the Art Students League in Manhattan. They were in a laundromat where he couldn't reach the change slot to start his wash. She helped him and they took it from there.

The first time they visit us on Thompson Street she brings a jar of home-made peach preserves. It is a typical gesture.

And Hervé. Looking like no other human being on the planet. A midget with the energy of a dynamo. The underdog's underdog. Aggressive, shy, tormented, creative, a perfectionist, alive with humor, native intelligence and imagination; he is a realist, an atheist, a socialist (philosophically), a capitalist (practically); he is a compulsive collector, a male chauvinist, a harsh critic of himself and others. He is courageous, cunning, ambitious, calculating, charming, and often depressed.

After knowing Hervé for a few months I realize that if he were normal size he would still be the most eccentric person I know. He is vocal in his dislike for phoniness—what he frequently refers to as "bullshit." In fact, he trusts very few people because of all the "bullshit" he's had to deal with. He bores easily and keeps his inner face well hidden behind an exterior of sardonic, black humor and hard work.

I've never seen anyone work as hard or as constantly as Hervé. He tackles the job of building his loft without regard for his small size. He hurries from one end to the other, carrying wood, rearranging tools, filing papers, always on the move. He's in motion even when sitting in a chair; a foot dangles nervously in the air, fingers drum on the nearest surface.

He is a romantic with an old-world sense of honor and chivalry. He might be more at home in an historic time when he could fight a duel with someone who slighted his dignity or the honor of someone he loved. He has great pride, specifying on his acting résumé—"No elves or Santa's Helper, please."

He knows how to live with little money and few possessions; he wastes nothing. His records of business dealings

9

and expenditures are meticulous, his sense of self-suffi-
ciency is total. He has infrequent communication with his
family in France and implies that they're happy he's no
longer in his homeland.

When we meet Hervé he is 27 years old. He sketches
pieces of his history for us without any show of self pity.

He is sixteen when he first comes to America on an art
scholarship. He speaks no English and learns the language
from cowboy westerns on TV while staying in a seedy midtown hotel. He witnesses street violence in all imaginable
forms and is deeply and permanently affected by the experience. His bourgeois, doctor's-son upbringing in Paris
and southern France now coexists with New York City concrete and blood reality. These two sides of Hervé are ex-
pressed at various times and in unusual ways during the
following years.

When we meet him in 1970 he has made only slight in-
roads into an acting career. There are few parts available
for midget actors but he is undeterred.

He gets a minor role in Norman Mailer's film *Maidstone*
and tells us after the filming that while on location he fell into
a swimming pool. Since he couldn't swim he called for help.
According to his retelling, Mailer shouted for lights and cameras, filmed Hervé flailing away in the water and finally had
him pulled, gasping, from the pool. When the film *Maidstone*
is released, Hervé's part is cut to a few close-ups of his
thick, small hands, playing a piano.

He tells us that people are always trying to take advantage
of him because of his size. "They see a midget," he says,
"and think I'm stupid. They're wrong."

That's for sure. Although he dropped out of school in
France when he was eleven years old, he is knowledgeable
in many disparate areas of life, from plumbing and construction to silver coins and antiques. His impulse is to repair or
build anything himself and this do-it-yourself attitude often
leads to accidents in his loft. He's been clobbered by falling
two-by-fours and his body is a network of scars from various

accidents. But he thrives on risks and lets nothing stand in his way.

Sandy and I greatly admire his fierce determination. Compared with the odds he's up against, our struggles seem minor indeed.

We live in Little Italy in a fifth floor walk-up apartment about five blocks from their loft on Greene Street. Our building looks out on another tenement with a half-dozen Italian women staring out their windows from various floors, watching their kids and small dogs play in the courtyard below. We fight a losing battle with cockroaches and our neighbors who don't feel right unless they're arguing violently. Whenever they argue we play Bob Dylan on our stereo. We listen to a lot of Dylan.

Sandy has a certain gentleness in common with Anne. Her heart-shaped face and angelic features suggest the same softness. Her China-blue eyes can change in feeling from "All-American" to exotic "Meet me in Hong Kong."

She is soft-spoken and rarely judgmental, serene and infinitely patient. These characteristics harmonize well with my more mercurial, action-oriented temperament.

She studies batik painting with an Indian Master, practices Tai Chi Chuan, is drawn to eastern philosophies and soon becomes a vegetarian. And I'm crazy about her.

I'm an activist in the antiwar movement, and an inveterate optimist. I share the struggles and dreams of the idealists of my generation, and am predisposed to question authority. The rebel in me is close friend with the rebel in Hervé. If I have any claim to fame it's because I've won over five hundred thumb-wrestling matches in a row. Occasionally, I wonder why my athletic prowess dwells in my thumbs.

Summer—1971

Anne and Hervé move from Greene Street to another loft nearby on Broadway. We help them with the move. With a few friends we dismantle the plasterboard wall they built and move their belongings by van to their new loft. "New loft" is certainly a euphemism. If ever a place could be described as "needs work" this is it. Their Broadway sixth floor space used to be a button factory. More recently it was used by silkscreen printers. The freight elevator opens onto a dimly lit floor, approximately seventy feet long and twenty feet wide. About a third of the space is cluttered by a wooden table piled high with hundreds of dusty old silkscreens that have been left behind. The eastern end of the floor has floor-to-ceiling windows which overlook Broadway. The western end has two heavy metal doors which open onto an equally spacious roof, covered with gravel and crushed buttons. There's not much of a kitchen, even less of a bathroom.

Anne and Hervé begin the Herculean task of clearing, building and repairing their loft, an effort that will take two years. It takes months for them to reduce the number of silkscreens. They catalog each one—selling some, giving others away and using the wood from the table to build a platform for an old-fashioned tub.

They do all the work themselves, partly because they don't have the money to hire workers and partly because Hervé can't see paying money for something he can do himself. They sand and varnish the wood floor, install plumbing, spend endless hours scraping and painting the dingy walls, and build a platform which they use for storage. They continue to collect street throwaways—oak desks, chairs, a green velvet couch (somewhat tattered but still elegant), a bright red coke machine from the fifties, an old cash register, a showcase for·their antique jewelry, a mannequin and anything else of possible value the streets have to offer for free.

Hervé frequents nearby Canal Street, a discount hardware mecca. He can't resist the low prices for odds and ends and impulsively buys buckets of the stuff. He lines their loft with Canal Street bargains, sometimes causing Anne to roll her eyes in disbelief. But she is very tolerant of his eccentricities.

They have barbeque parties on their rooftop soon after moving in. And their loft slowly takes shape. They furnish the roof with a table, chairs and a white porcelain toilet filled with earth and blooming flowers. At parties we often sit around the table, drink wine and watch the sun set in back of a skyline of watertowers.

But Anne grows increasingly unhappy about living in New York City, as does Sandy. They're bothered more than Hervé and I by the pollution, the harsh life, the noise and concrete.

During one discussion about New York City, Hervé points to a window in the factory building overlooking their roof. "That's a bathroom window," he says. "You know what they do up there? They throw their used Tampax and toilet paper onto our roof. It's disgusting. I'm collecting all their garbage in a large carton and when it's full I'm going to take it up there and empty it all on the foreman's desk."

We don't doubt that he will. He seems to have a violent, wild streak that remains in check at least most of the time.

Fall—1972

Sandy and I move from our Thompson Street apartment to a more elegant place in Greenwich Village—a four room floor-through with plenty of light. Our rent triples and in the coming months so do the number of our possessions.

Anne and Hervé help with the move, packing books and records, and giving moral support. None of us can think of a good reason why we all continue to live in New York City. But with a philosophical shrug we all continue to do just that.

Sandy and I both sense that Anne's and Herve's relationship is changing. Hervé seems restless and less patient with Anne. Nothing's discussed. It's just a feeling.

We celebrate the completed move at 1 a.m. with a round of omelets in a local restaurant. They wish us luck and we return to our new home. We marvel at the improvement. Our new apartment has the look of an old French hotel. It has parquet floors, an elaborate marble fireplace, a separate kitchen with a window, and tall, narrow doors that open to a rooftop overlooking the tree-filled courtyard where E. E. Cummings wrote much of his poetry. We wonder if we've found a home at last in the city.

We don't wonder for long. Within a few days it becomes apparent that we're living in one of the noisiest sections of town. Fire engines wail out of the firehouse across the street. Ambulances shriek past our window toward St. Vincent's Hospital, around the corner. And several subway lines run into the West 4th Street Station several hundred vibrating feet beneath our floor.

I consider lining the entire apartment with cork. Suddenly I understand why so many people in New York talk to themselves.

It isn't long before I share Sandy's feelings about Manhattan. "What the hell are we doing here?" I ask after a few months. "We're both country people."

We plot our escape as do Hervé and Anne. But we're plotting for different reasons. By spring it's apparent that their relationship is deteriorating. Hervé mentions to me that he wants to be free to sleep with other women. He says he's suggested to Anne that she sleep with other men. He talks of the tension that exists between them.

14

Hervé wearing a belt buckle as glasses, 1973

It's painful to see what's happening to them. They've struggled together for years, and now, just when Hervé has had some success with roles in the movies *The Gang That Couldn't Shoot Straight* and *Greaser's Palace,* they're on the skids.

They decide to go to Paris. We decide to go to Norway. "Enough is enough," we tell each other. We store our "things," as we now call them, and prepare for our trip. We buy sleeping bags and backpacks and maps of Norway.

The four of us leave for Paris and Norway within a few weeks of each other. Our farewell is sad but intimate. Anne and Hervé throw a small party on their roof during which we're acutely aware that a stage in our friendship is over. Whatever the future holds will be different, significantly different, from what we've known these past three years.

We fly to Norway and live in shepherds' huts in the mountains for a few months, painting, writing, photographing. As fall approaches, our money runs low and with a Norwegian winter closing in, we decide to return to the States.

We stop in Paris and visit with Anne before flying to New York. She tells us that Hervé has returned to their loft in New York and she's decided to stay in the apartment they recently leased for $60 a month near the Eiffel Tower. She wants to learn French. Suddenly she's on her own, expressing ambivalent feelings about her situation. She misses Hervé but says that their relationship has become rocky. He wants to see other women and she's still in love with him and finds it impossible to accept his demands. She talks about how difficult he has made it for them to live together in peace. All of this depresses her but at the same time she is exhilarated by her sudden independence. She's on her own in Paris and that has a certain appealing ring to her.

She asks where we're going to live when we return to the States. We tell her we're not sure—maybe someplace in New England. Maybe New Mexico. She tells us how much she and Hervé liked Santa Fe, New Mexico when they were filming *Greaser's Palace* there. We say we'll keep it in mind.

16

As we talk it becomes apparent just how much our lives have changed in a few months. We share our recent experiences in a half-dozen cafes and bars during the few days we're in Paris. And this time it's a tearful farewell in the métro. We know it will be some time before we see each other again.

Sandy and I take a plane to New York and spend several weeks driving through the New England countryside, scouting for a place to live. We move into a cottage in Shady, a small town near Woodstock, New York, and spend the winter there.

Mid-winter, we receive a letter from Anne, in Paris. She describes her painful separation from Hervé, his subsequent hospitalization for a failing kidney, and their indecision about whether to keep their Soho loft. Anne writes that Hervé's out of the hospital now, depressed and living in their loft. She ends her letter: "I just want us to get out of N.Y. especially with his health, being nervous and afraid and asphyxiated doesn't help. Please Scott and Sandy try with me to convince him to give it up and we can take something together in Woodstock or try to work out something to live together in the states."

I phone Hervé and ask if he'd like to spend some time with us. He says he'd love to. The following morning I drive into New York City and buzz for him at his loft. He steps onto his fire escape and waves down to me. Ten minutes later we're driving out of the city.

It's great to see each other again. We discuss old times and new times. He talks about how difficult things got with Anne. "She has to learn to live on her own. I don't know what will happen between us."

During the ride to Shady he also says that he's been thinking about writing his autobiography or having someone write his biography. I tell him I'm still unpublished but if he decides to have someone write his biography I'd like to do it.

He thinks that's a good idea. We're both searching for

ways to make some money and a book about his life seems like a good project for both of us. He says he'll send letters and notes about his life for me to read.

As we approach the Suffern, New York exit I notice that Hervé is having difficulty breathing. He clutches his chest and gasps for air.

"What's wrong? You O.K.?"

He kneels on the front seat, presses his hands to his heart and shakes his head. He's sweating and obviously in pain.

I turn off the highway at the Suffern exit and race into town. I park in front of a police station, run in, and ask the officer on duty, "Can you tell me where the nearest hospital is? I've got a midget in my car and he can't breathe."

The police officer's eyes widen. "Up the street about a mile and a half. You want an escort?"

"No, thanks." I rush out the door to the car, speed to the hospital and help Hervé walk into the emergency room. After signing in, he's led to a curtained cubicle and his blood pressure is taken. It's high. They give him an injection. "A muscle relaxer," the doctor tells me.

Hervé lies down on an examining table and in about twenty minutes his intense stomach cramp eases and he's able to breathe more normally. He's observed for another hour and when he says he's feeling better, the doctor tells him he can go home.

Before we leave, one of the nurses asks, "Weren't you in the movie *The Gang That Couldn't Shoot Straight?*"

He nods weakly.

"You were great in it," she beams.

We continue our drive to Shady, arriving late in the afternoon. After some hot soup and quiet catching up, Hervé goes into the room we've made up for him and disappears for the night.

"Do you think he'll be O.K.?" Sandy asks.

"I don't know. It was really intense when he had the attack in the car."

18

He feels much better the following morning after a good night's sleep. He tells us he'd like to see the countryside. Snow has fallen during the night and it looks inviting outside. We have breakfast and I ask Hervé if he'd like to make a ½" videotape with us at a place called Clarence's Sculpture Garden.

"Who was Clarence?" he asks.

"According to stories we've heard in Shady," I tell him, "Clarence was a brilliant, eccentric, artist/anarchist who created his life's work on his property in front of his cabin. The cabin is abandoned now and falling apart."

"What happened to Clarence?"

"According to the stories, a few years ago he was put in a state institution after walking naked through the center of town."

Hervé likes Clarence's Sculpture Garden already. "Sure," he says, "let's make a videotape there. It sounds interesting."

We carry my video equipment to the car and slide it onto the back seat. It's about thirty degrees and overcast. We drive through the back roads of Woodstock until we come upon a driveway sloping toward Clarence's Sculpture Garden. We park, carry the video equipment to the garden entrance, and rest it on the snow-covered ground. We wander silently through the sculpture garden of Clarence's mind: rows of baby dolls without clothing or hair, mannequin heads with silver balls for eyes, plastic flowers, aluminum foil lining the branches of trees, the grill of a fifties Buick embedded in a hillside, hubcaps welded into auto sculpture with steering wheels, beercan edifices, shattered mirrors, a smashed TV, an altar-like collage of photos from the Kennedy assassination. And in the middle of all this? Clarence's dilapidated cabin without a front door or glass in the windows.

Hervé is mesmerized. He's never seen an artist's work as similar in spirit to his own. He's drawn to the baby dolls in particular and comments on the crate full of similar baby dolls that he has in his loft.

19

We set up the video equipment. I improvise a script and shoot for an hour, while a dog barks incessantly in the distance.

We leave Clarence's Sculpture Garden, electrified by the experience. This is the first time we've worked together creatively and we're buzzing. We return to the cottage and our excitement grows when we play the tape back through our TV. "Very beautiful," Hervé comments. "Very sensitive. I like the way you shot this."

When he returns to the city he feels fine. Creative work is a balm for his edgy moods. Our friendship gains a new dimension. And a few weeks later I receive in the mail a packet of love letters written by Hervé and ex-girlfriends. I read them reluctantly, knowing they weren't written with my eyes or publication in mind. I'm startled by how ordinary they seem.

"It's amazing," I tell Sandy. "There's nothing in these letters that doesn't sound like a TV soap opera." I put the letters away and receive another packet several weeks later. I don't know what to do with them. They're rambling descriptions about tangled love affairs, reading like clichés. I shelve the project and return everything to him when he asks about the letters.

Early Spring—1973

Our lease is up on the cottage in Shady, and before we know it we're back in Manhattan, searching for an apartment and jobs. We're stunned and frustrated to be back in the city but we don't have the money to start touring the country for another place to live.

Shortly after returning to the city we get a phone call from Hervé. Anne is returning from Paris. He asks if we'd drive

20

him to the airport to pick her up. We say we'd love to. We feel better about Manhattan already.

Late Spring—1973

We drive Hervé to Kennedy Airport. He's nervous about Anne's coming back. "I want my freedom," he says, swigging from a bottle of wine. We have a beer at an airport bar and he photographs a rainbow arcing a plane on the runway.

Anne finally emerges from customs, looking as nervous as Hervé. He insists that he sit in back of our car and she sit up front. He tells her we're driving directly to their friends, Simon and Eleanor, on Long Island. "We're all going to a flea market tomorrow morning," he says. We're surprised he hasn't mentioned our plan to her during a phone conversation before her flight. His icy reception toward her continues until the following day.

We sleep in sleeping bags that night on the floor of Simon's and Eleanor's house and the next morning the four of us drive to the flea market. Our trunk is full of antiques we've gathered separately. We set up two card tables and display our wares. Hervé is selling some old bottles, cameras, daguerreotypes, antique jewelry and a silver-and-turquoise bracelet he bought in Santa Fe. He takes no chances with the more valuable bracelet, tying it to a chain which is secured to the table.

Sandy and I are offering a silver pickle jar, several New England crocks, a cut glass bowl, a brass knocker and a miniature tea set.

Business is slow and it looks like rain. Just before the skies open, a stocky man with a thin moustache stops in front of Hervé's table. "You ever race a horse?"

"No."

21

The man looks him up and down several times. "What's your weight? Under ninety pounds, right?"

Hervé nods.

"Well, there you have it. I'm a horse trainer at Aqueduct. You could be a great jockey, you know it?" He thrusts a meaty right hand in front of Hervé. "Squeeze my hand," he says.

Hervé looks at the man's hand.

"Go ahead, squeeze it. I want to see how strong you are."

Hervé squeezes the man's hand.

"Not bad," the man says, "not bad at all. You got some strength." He writes his name and telephone number on a piece of paper and hands it to Hervé. "Call me if you wanna be a jockey. You'll make good money, for sure."

Hervé tells him he'll think it over.

"You do that."

Hervé laughs at the thought of becoming a jockey. He fantasizes about it but cuts short his fantasy with, "No, I can't be a jockey. One bad fall and I'd be through."

It starts to rain and we quickly pack our antiques and card tables into our Buick and head toward Manhattan. On the way the four of us discuss the possibility of selling antiques together. Hervé and Anne suggest their loft as a location for the business.

And so we start an informal antique business called The Soho Loft. We put living room antiques in their living room, kitchen antiques in their kitchen, thereby opening up their entire loft for customer browsing.

The Soho Loft is launched when Hervé and I put together an ad for the business. Hervé draws caricatures of the four of us grinning from ear to ear, and I write the copy. Within a week the ad, suggestive of Charles Addams and the Marx Brothers, is taped to mailboxes and streetlamps from lower to upper Manhattan.

We spend much of our spare time buying stock. Responding to ads in "The Village Voice," we purchase unusual period pieces for little money. But it soon becomes apparent that we're spending too much time running around the city, buying a few antiques here, a few there.

With this in mind, Hervé and I go to Brooklyn to an address given in a "Village Voice" ad for a "fantastic" one-day garage sale. We buy over a hundred dollars of bric-a-brac: two forties strollers, several kitchen scales, a hand-painted bread box, a two-faced cookie jar, a crate of old bottles, a tin pretzel container, and dozens of odd tools, perfume bottles, and sundries of earlier generations.

We pay the delighted man, fill the two strollers with our purchases, and load the car. When we wheel the two strollers off the elevator into the loft, Sandy's and Anne's laughter greets us. We show what we've bought like it was Christmas morning.

Business is slow, but stray tourists, adventurers, and dealers who respond to our ad are rewarded by a rich experience. The elevator doors open to the crooning of one of Hervé's childhood French singer/heroes playing on a twenties victrola. Hervé, holding a china teacup, examines the bottom of the cup and then clinks it against his teeth, listening to the ring to demonstrate quality. Some customers double-take Hervé when they step off the elevator. Others pretend they expected no less. They browse through the loft the way book lovers browse through bookstores looking for first editions. They take their time and are respectful of what they handle.

"Welcome," one of us calls. There's a friendly, informal atmosphere. We discuss the particulars of anything with anyone who asks. Some buy. Most just look. Dealers usually select six or eight items and make a ridiculously low bid on them. We counter with a high bid. Sometimes we settle. Most often we don't.

Later, we lock the door and go out on the roof. We sit at the table, drink wine, talk over the day and watch the sun set behind the watertowers.

Unfortunately, The Soho Loft is ahead of its time in concept and behind its time in financing. By the following spring,

23

our business is about breaking even. And Anne and Hervé are about breaking up. The four of us take steps to end our joint venture. They're making plans to move to Paris again. We're making plans to go to Mexico. We all vow not to return to Manhattan.

Hervé has had success of sorts recently with a role in the James Bond film *The Man With The Golden Gun.* He feels he'll be able to get work in Paris as an actor, now that he has some fame in the United States.

Anne and Hervé sell their loft, getting back the money they put into it but nothing for their two years of hard labor. They swear they'll never do all the heavy work in a loft again. "Next time," Hervé says, "I'll hire people."

They leave for Paris around the same time that we store our possessions and drive to San Miguel de Allende, Mexico. We spend two years getting our Master of Fine Arts degrees in painting and creative writing. During this time we correspond with Anne. She stays in Paris. But Herve,' unable to find work in France, returns to the U.S. and goes to Hollywood. They've split up and there's no indication in Anne's letters that she wants to be with him. Her letters glow with new-found liberation. She has a lover, a job, and a sense of herself that she never had when she was with Hervé. She writes that it could never work again between them because he was "too cruel, too violent and too egotistical."

Fall—1976

We leave San Miguel de Allende. We've had a rewarding two years in Mexico and we're hopeful that we'll be able to teach and continue to paint and write. But we run headlong into the economic reality of the seventies—many applicants for few college jobs preferentially given to those with teaching experience.

In frustration, we wind up in Manhattan again. "We swore we'd never move back," Sandy says as we move into a studio on lower Fifth Avenue.

"We'll stay only until we find something," I console. "It won't be bad. The rent's low. It's got southern exposure. It's quiet. It's got a great view of the World Trade Center."

"And it's one room, 12′ × 17′."

I work as a substitute teacher and Sandy works four days a week for an ad agency. Much of her free time is spent in a shared Soho loft where she builds lightboxes for her batiks and works toward having a show.

Fall—1977

I have a series of black and white photographs of sand formations taken on the western coast of Mexico. They're dramatic abstracts and Sandy and I envision them as a photo book.

I show the series to one publisher who asks to see additional photographs. It's possible that a photo book of sand formations would fit in nicely with the "pattern" books they publish.

I phone the Museum of Natural History and describe the photos. I also talk with someone in the Geology Department at Rutgers University. Where in the United States can I find similar formations? I learn that I have been photographing "rhomboids" and a good place to look for them would be off the coast of North Carolina around Hattaras, and Death Valley, California.

During this time Hervé phones us and says he's in town

for the opening of an underground film he's in called *Hot Tomorrows*. He describes it as "a very heavy film, about death."

He's staying in the apartment of a vacationing friend, a few blocks from where we live. We visit with him several times and he's in the best physical and emotional shape we've ever seen him. In fact, he seems like a changed man. He's less nervous and more at peace with himself. When we get together now, it's as old, dear friends.

We go with him to the opening of *Hot Tomorrows* at the New York Film Festival and to several parties, and he fills us in on his life since he moved to L.A. He describes his struggle to survive during the first year there, sleeping in cars in the Hollywood hills when necessary. He had no money and knew few people. But he did know what to do. He used to dress like a Hollywood movie star and go to a bar called Joe Allen's with beautiful actresses. They were certain to be noticed in his company and he was certain to be noticed in theirs. His strategy paid off. He got one of the best Hollywood agents to represent him and he landed a part in a movie starring Henry Winkler called *The One And Only*.

Now, he tells us, his career is really taking off. He's going to be co-starring in a TV series called "Fantasy Island," to be aired in a few months. After eighteen years of struggling with little money, he's signed a solid, long-term contract with ABC. His elation is tempered only by his regret that his relationship with Anne has broken off. She's stopped corresponding from Paris and apparently doesn't want anything to do with him. His lawyer in L.A. is about to initiate divorce proceedings.

He admits he treated Anne badly, even cruelly. But, he explains, there were reasons for his cruelty. She wasn't prepared to live in the "real" world by herself. She'd led too sheltered a life. He had to teach her what life was really like. Now he's sorry for what he put her through, but it's too late to do anything about it.

26

Sandy and I listen without commenting about his non-relationship with Anne. Her recent letters to us have been highly critical of him. We do tell him how much we miss Anne, though.

"She's changed," he replies. "She's not the same Anne you knew when we lived in Soho. She's much harder now. She doesn't write to any of her friends in New York anymore."

Sandy mentions that she's been corresponding with Anne and Hervé seems stunned. "Really?" he says. "What does she say? Does she write about me?"

Sandy is evasive, protecting Anne. "She sounds like she's in good shape. She enjoys living in Paris and the freedom of her new life."

"Does she mention me?"

"Only in passing."

Hervé tells us several times how surprised he is that Anne is still writing to us. "She's not writing to anyone else in New York," he repeats. His interest in us seems further kindled. He asks what we've been doing since we returned from Mexico.

Sandy talks about the batik lightboxes she's constructed. He asks if he could see them and they arrange a time to meet, the following day.

I show Hervé the photos of sand formations and tell of the publisher's interest in them as a book. He loves the photos and thinks they'd make a great book. He's supportive and complimentary.

The following day he meets Sandy. She shows him the batik lightboxes and his response is enthusiastic. He tells her that if he had one of her lightboxes in his house he'd hang it in his bedroom and leave the lights on all the time.

Before leaving for Los Angeles, he suggests that we travel west for a visit. He knows many writers, photographers and painters and would introduce us. "You can stay at my house," he says. "I'm sure you could sell your work in Los Angeles."

27

I tell him that we plan a trip to North Carolina soon to photograph sand formations and that Death Valley, California has been suggested as another possible location for similar photos.

"Good. Just give me a call."

He returns to Los Angeles and later we drive to North Carolina in search of rhomboids. We find extraordinary rhomboids near Hattaras but wonder if we have enough variety for a book. I decide to go to Death Valley to get more.

I phone Hervé and tell him I'll be arriving in L.A. at two o'clock the following morning. He's as excited as I am and says he'll leave the key to the front door under a flower pot on the porch.

3:30 a.m. and I'm standing in front of Hervé's two-story house. I find the key, make my way inside to a couch and fall asleep.

I'm awakened a few hours later by one of Hervé's roommates crashing about the kitchen. Before I can fall asleep again he wheels an enormous black motorcycle through the living room, out the front door and down the front steps. He roars off into the smog.

Welcome to L.A. I forget about sleep and gaze about the room. The largest objects, now that the motorcycle is gone, are several marimbas.

An hour later, Hervé comes down the staircase which ends at the foot of the couch. He's wearing a pair of cut-off jeans and nothing else. His eyes are half-closed with sleep. We embrace hello and he heads straight for the kitchen, mumbling, "Coffee." He fills his espresso machine with fine Mexican coffee and as soon as the smell fills the air he comes alive. A few sips of the muddy stuff and he's humming with energy.

We talk about his show, "Fantasy Island." It's a fast-breaking hit and the changes it's carving into his life are considerable. Suddenly, he's being asked on talk shows and is investing his money through a business manager. He has a speech therapist, a driver, and his own trailer on the set.

28

All this and he's still living in a roach-infested house in a rundown part of town.

The calm Hervé we saw a few months before in Manhattan is gone. His sudden fame and wealth are accompanied by serious dislocations of former ways of life. Everywhere he goes now, people recognize him. And they won't leave him alone.

He sips his espresso and tells me of a recent incident on the street. A man forced him into a car and took him home to meet "the wife and kids." He was then driven back to the street where he had been accosted. I laugh but empathize with the loss of freedom caused by his fame.

He shows me the garden he's planted in his backyard. And he leads me upstairs and shows me his office and then the bedroom, which contains a four-foot pyramid of beer cans. "An early warning system for earthquakes," he notes. He introduces me to Suzanne, a former girlfriend recently arrived from Denmark and staying with him.

During the following week I'm chauffeured with Hervé to the Burbank Studios set where "Fantasy Island" is produced. I meet his speech therapist, wardrobe attendant, driver, and others in his Hollywood retinue. He introduces me to Ricardo Montalban, his co-star, and later tells me that Ricardo is very conservative. "He won't fight for the rights of the crew. He's afraid to take risks. I always fight for the crew. Ricardo likes things just the way they are."

Early the following morning I'm with Hervé and Suzanne in his trailer. There's a knock on the trailer door.

"Come in," Hervé calls.

A driver named Ed steps into the trailer and is introduced to Suzanne and me. We shake hands and I think — this guy's really drunk, and it's only seven-thirty in the morning.

Ed kids with Hervé and before long pulls a revolver from his jacket. We're all taken aback by the sight of the gun. Ed laughs and waves it casually in the air.

"It's not loaded," he says. He playfully points the gun at Suzanne, and then at me. He drops his aim and squeezes the trigger. A flash of orange shoots from the gun's barrel and a bullet explodes into the shag rug.

"Ho!" Ed steps back and stares at the gun. "Sorry about that. I guess it *was* loaded."

We're too shaken to respond. Ed exits quickly, after saying he'd appreciate it if we kept the incident to ourselves.

Despite the loud gunshot, no one comes to Herve's trailer to investigate. "They probably think someone's filming a western on the set," Hervé comments. He digs his fingers into the rug and finds the spent bullet, its nose now pug. "I want to keep this as a reminder. This is how close death was to us." He pockets the bullet, finds the casing nearby, and hands it to me. "Keep it, as your reminder." I slip the casing into my trucker's wallet and focus my thinking on getting out of L.A. and to Death Valley.

I tell Hervé on Thursday that I'll be renting a car and driving to Death Valley. Would he like to come along and do some photographing? He'd like to but he has a date in San Francisco this weekend.

Friday morning I'm downstairs talking with Suzanne, when the phone rings. It's Herve, calling from upstairs. "Come on up here. I want to talk with you."

I walk upstairs and he's pacing back and forth in his office. "I'm going to Death Valley with you," he announces, grinning. "I just made up my mind. I was all set to go to San Francisco when I thought—why spend a weekend with Barbara? She's trouble. I haven't spent time with Scott in years and he may not be back for a long time. So I decided—I'm going with you."

I'm delighted. "Great! When do you want to leave?"

"As early as possible tomorrow morning—which means we have plenty to do. We have to buy film...get our things together...clothing, supplies, an extra can of gasoline...."

We're like two kids preparing for a camping trip, as we scurry about for money, cameras, tripods, clothing and food.

We rent a car and go to a party that night. Leaving the party around one in the morning, on the drive back to Nor-

30

mandie Avenue, we simultaneously have the same idea: let's get our stuff together and head out now.

We pack our gear and are ready to leave by 3:00 a.m. equipped with a thermos of hot coffee, a small camping stove, a sleeping bag, cameras, tripods, filters, a bag of film, and a few hundred dollars between us.

We drive out of L.A. on a highway thick with fog, unable to go more than ten miles per hour. Craning our necks toward the windshield, we strain to locate the dividing line. The fog lifts after about an hour's crawl and we speed through the chilly night toward Death Valley.

Drinking coffee and buzzing with energy, Hervé turns on the radio, takes out his harmonica and wails along with whatever song happens to be playing.

We drive to the Mohave Desert's edge and stop at a roadside cafe. It's 5:00 a.m.

"Feels great to be heading toward Death Valley," I say.

He agrees. "I needed to get out of Los Angeles. The pressure was getting to me."

We walk into the cafe. A young woman, wearing a name tag "Sherry" on her white uniform, looks at Hervé. "Aren't you the guy on that show 'Fantasy Island'?"

Hervé grins. "We'd like two cheese omelets."

"Holy cow!" she exclaims. "Can I have your autograph?" She opens the door to the kitchen and shouts, "Hey Tommy! You got a piece of paper? The midget from 'Fantasy Island' is out here."

Tommy, a pimply-faced, lanky teenager, pokes his head out the door. "Hey—you're Tattoo on 'Fantasy Island,' right?"

Hervé smiles. "Are you the cook?"

He steps up to us and says, "Sure am. What'll it be?"

"Two cheese omelets," Sherry says.

"That it?"

"And toast. You have rye bread?"

"Rye bread?" the cook repeats. "No rye bread. White and whole wheat."

31

"Whole wheat," Hervé says.

"Same for you?"

I nod and say, "I'm Tattoo's driver."

The cook rushes back to the kitchen and Sherry pushes a napkin and pen in front of Hervé. "Can I have your autograph?"

Hervé signs his name and draws a heart with an arrow through it.

"You want the autograph of the driver of Hervé?" I ask.

Sherry doesn't want to hurt my feelings. "Sure," she says. She passes the pen to me and on another napkin I scribble "Scott—Driver of Hervé." She thanks me and we sit down in a booth.

Sherry arrives with two elastic cheese omelets, "Made special for ya by Tommy. He says he'd like an autograph too, after you eat his omelets."

As the first light of morning touches the desert night we leave the cafe and continue toward Death Valley, Hervé playing his harmonica to the music of early morning radio. Our close friendship has come alive again. On the road, beyond the show biz haze of Hollywood, he's like he used to be—filled with wonder and the feeling that everything on and about the planet is miraculous from any height.

The sun rises and we drive for hours before stopping in the parking lot of a small-town supermarket. We stretch our legs and enter the supermarket as it opens at nine. Herve's entrance causes a stir. Employees point and dash off to tell their friends. We wheel a cart up and down the aisles, stocking up for the trip: dried cereals, oranges, bananas, nuts, dried fruit, bread.

A young man behind a meat counter spots Hervé and leaps over the counter saying, "It's you! It's you! Let me shake your hand, Tattoo!"

Soon we're surrounded by autograph seekers.

"Let's get out of here," Hervé says.

We check out quickly and are on the road again. "That blew my mind," Hervé says several times during the next half hour. "Did you see that? I had no idea the shc so popular."

We joke about his reception and drive into the California desert. I've been driving for seven straight hours and my lids are getting mighty heavy. I head down a mountain road and doze off for a split second. The car veers, I awaken, turn the steering wheel sharply, and hear Hervé gasp, all at the same moment. He clutches his chest at our close call.

"Sorry," I say. "How about some more coffee?"

"If my agent knew I was making this trip he'd really freak out. He doesn't want me to do *any*thing. There are rules written into my contract with ABC. I'm not even supposed to fly in a plane without their permission."

We reach Death Valley around eleven in the morning and begin our search for rhomboids and near cousins. We drive another five hours in 100 plus heat, but we don't find any sand formations similar in feeling or content to the ones I photographed off the shores of North Carolina and Mexico.

By late afternoon, we're exhausted. We've been driving for fifteen straight hours. As the sun sets, we drive into town to check into a motel. But the town's two motels are full. While wondering where we're going to sleep tonight we're approached by two tall, skinny, blonde young men. They recognize Hervé and want to shake his hand. We talk for a while. They're sweet kids.

"Motels full up, huh?" one of them says before they leave.

We nod.

"Where you guys gonna sleep tonight?"

We shrug.

One of them says, "I'm thinking 'bout sleeping in that Conestoga wagon over there—the one advertising the motel."

"I'm sleeping back there where the cars are," the other says.

Hervé and I leave them and walk into a motel bar to talk things over. It's now about nine at night. We order beers and sit down at a table.

A group of young men drinking at a nearby table suddenly laugh uproariously. "That's him!" one of them insists. "I know that's him!"

"Ain't him," another says. "Bet you five it ain't him."

"You're on."

One man gets up and walks toward us. It's a wonder he can stand at all. "Hey," he says to Hervé, "s'cuse me and all but we're just havin' argument 'bout whether you're that midget whatsisname on TV."

The waitress brings our beers and Hervé tells the staggering questioner, "I don't like people betting on me. I'm not an animal." He softens, "Besides, when a bet is made on me I want part of the action."

"Sure, sure," the man says, "but y'are that midget on TV, aren't ya?"

Hervé nods and the man slaps his thighs and whoops "Hot damn!" He laughs and shouts to his friend, "Y'owe me five bucks. It's him, all right." Returning to his table he orders two drinks for us. His cronies laugh boisterously.

When the drinks arrive Hervé says, "We'll leave their drinks on the table."

We finish our beers and leave the bar amid catcalls of "Hey, Tattoo! Hey c'mere, Tattoo!"

We get into our car and I say, "Let's get out of here. I didn't like that scene in there."

Hervé by now is asleep and snoring, sitting in the front seat.

"Hey, Hervé," I say, "wake up. Come on. We've got to decide where we're sleeping tonight." I notice that our gas tank is a hair above *E.* "Hervé," I call, "wake up! We don't have much gas and the gas stations are closed for the night. Hervé!"

No use. I shake him but he doesn't wake up. I decide we have to get out of town regardless of how little gas is left in the tank. I'm concerned that the drunks will leave the bar and spot us in the car. I drive out of town, looking for a place to hide the car. About five miles away I find a dirt road leading off the highway, obscured from view by a sheltering hillside. I back down the rutted road until I'm out of sight, then turn off the engine and headlights.

I look at Herve, who sits peacefully fast asleep. I'm so exhausted I'm fighting nausea. Why can't I fall asleep? Come on. Mind over matter.

I close my eyes but can't relax. I'm afraid I'll topple forward in my sleep and smash headfirst into the steering wheel.

My quandary is interrupted when Hervé keels over from his sitting position and falls onto my lap. He stays tight asleep. I lift him off my lap and prop him upright against the door. I shake him hard, and speak into his ear. "Herve. This is Scott. Wake up. We've got a problem."

He mumbles unintelligibly in his sleep.

"I can't sleep in a car like this," I say out loud. "I've been in this seat driving for nineteen hours. I've got to get some sleep."

I turn the ignition key, flick the headlights on, and drive back onto the highway. Another five miles and fortune smiles: a rest area. I park the car, take my sleeping bag out of my suitcase and spread a worn army blanket on the macadam near the wheels of the car. I put my shoes in the back seat and Hervé coughs. He's roused enough to say, "Where are we?"

"Death Valley. We're at a rest area. I'll be outside in my sleeping bag. You can stretch out and have the front seat now."

He shakes his head and squints out the window. Then he grabs a blanket from his duffle bag, spreads it across the front seat, locks the doors, and stretches out for the night.

I slip into my sleeping bag and stare at the bowl of Death Valley stars. It's a chilly night at six thousand feet above sea level and before drifting off to sleep I wonder if frost is forming on my nose.

I awaken with the first light of an overcast day. My nose feels like it's shot full of novocaine. I slide out of my sleeping bag and realize that my shoes are locked in the car with

35

Herve: I rap on the window and door closest to his head. He slowly stirs and sits up, rubs his eyes and looks around him.

"Death Valley," I say to him. "Roll down the window. My shoes are in the back seat."

He rolls down the window. "Good morning." He stretches the kinks from his body. "I feel like a pretzel."

"Good morning," I reply, unlocking and opening the door. "I'm frozen." I put my shoes on. "You hungry?"

He nods. "Let's have some coffee." Rummaging through the back seat he finds his small camping stove and the thermos which still has coffee in it. He lights the stove on the hood of the car and heats the coffee in an aluminum pan. The coffee does wonders for us both, revitalizing our spirit of high adventure. "I haven't been this relaxed in months," Hervé exults. "I'm a happy midget."

After the coffee he walks with a roll of toilet paper over the hilly terrain. He returns shaking his head. "I couldn't find a safe place to go. Too many snake holes out there."

The first order of business is to transfer the spare five gallons of gas into the tank. Hervé takes the gas can out of the trunk of the car and howls "Damn it! They forgot to give me a funnel or something to pour the gas into the tank."

We're beginning to feel like a Laurel and Hardy movie. We stand just off the highway and wave down a passing car. Luckily, the driver has a funnel.

We drive another ten miles and suddenly I smell something burning. I pull over, stop, and open the hood. Smoke spews from the engine. I check the oil level and it's almost empty. We open two cans of oil but can't find where to pour it. We search the engine thoroughly, then flag down another car. The driver searches for several minutes before saying, "Well, I'll be...here it is. Behind this pollution device." We pour the oil in, thank him, and are on our way.

We descend slowly to sea level and are struck by the breathtaking beauty of one particular spot. I stop the car and we get out the cameras, tripods, film and filters and separate.

"I'm a happy midget!" Death Valley

I photograph sand formations and Hervé photographs the landscape. Although we spend over an hour in different locations, we return to the car simultaneously. We're in perfect sync.

"I'm a happy midget!" he shouts. "Yahoo!"

We pack our gear into the car and are off again, heading toward L.A., feeling on top of the world. During the drive, Hervé tells me he's thinking about buying a house in the country outside of L.A.

"I'd like Sandy and you to live with me in my new house."

I look at him to see if he's serious. He is. "I don't know," I tell him. "I've got a job waiting for me in New York. And Sandy has a job working for a publisher. It would be tough to give that up. We've been looking for work for a long time."

Hervé persists. "You could get work in Los Angeles as a writer. It might take a few months but it would happen."

I muse on the idea. Move to L.A.? Become a Hollywood writer? "I don't know," I repeat. "You really think I could break through as a writer?"

"Yes, I know a lot of people out here. I could introduce you to them. And I've been thinking. I really like your photographs of sand formations. I'd like to publish them as a book myself."

Again I look to see if he's serious. Again, he is.

"What job will you have in New York?"

"I'll be working as a writer for a list broker."

"What do they do?"

"They rent and manage lists of names of mail order customers."

He shakes his head in disbelief. "You're an artist. Why do you want to work in an office? It's so boring."

"It's not that I *want* to work in an office. I have no choice. It's the only job I could come up with after months of looking. The job market is really tight these days."

"If you move to L.A. I can introduce you to people who can help you get work. Look, I have my selfish reasons for wanting you to live with me. But I also want to help you and

38

Sandy. You could write for 'Fantasy Island'—you should see the crap that's written now."

I tell him I'll discuss the idea with Sandy when I get back to New York.

"I'm serious about this," he adds.

I consider his offer during the return to L.A. I don't look forward to working in Manhattan for a list broker. In L.A. I could write for television. Sandy would have time and space to do her work. And we could live with Hervé without getting in each other's way. He has his dark moods but he's never imposed them on us.

By the time we arrive at his house we're bubbling with high spirits from our trip. I spend a few more days with him. He introduces me to a writer and a photographer, and he takes my recently completed novel to his agent's assistant.

During these final days in L.A., Suzanne asks me if I know if Hervé is trying to drive her out of his house.

"He hasn't mentioned anything to me."

"He's so cold and critical. He watches every move I make. He's driving me crazy."

I tell her, "The only thing he's said is that you should buy some California clothing so he can take you places." Suzanne looks like a fifties beatnik in her worn jeans, sandals, sweater and brown bomber's jacket.

Later, Hervé tells me that he doesn't want to get involved with Suzanne. "She doesn't really like to fuck," he says. "I like a woman who really likes to fuck."

The night before I return to New York, I'm with Herve, Suzanne and his speech therapist in his trailer on the set. He's smoking a cigar and feeling blue. He tells me, "I miss you already and you're not even gone yet." He opens a bottle of wine and fills four plastic cups. "I want you and Sandy to move out here," he says. "I really do." He removes a manuscript from a drawer and says, "This is a children's story I wrote. It needs to be rewritten. Would you like to hear it as it is?"

He reads a story about a man who became very rich and

wound up living alone in a big house. Because the man wasn't loving or generous, his life was empty and unhappy.

The story isn't as poignant or human as the feeling that exists in the trailer when he finishes reading. It's pure love.

I reach for the bottle of wine for a refill and suddenly the mood breaks. Hervé looks at me critically. What the hell's wrong, I wonder.

We return to the house and Suzanne takes me aside and says, "He watches every move we make. Did you see how he looked at you after you poured yourself the wine?"

"Yeah, but I can't get uptight about it. Hervé and I are old friends. I feel comfortable enough around him to dispense with social bullshit."

We walk into the kitchen and see Hervé fuming by the stove. He yanks a frying pan off a burner and says, "God-damn it! I told them to clean up after they eat. Roaches are crawling all over the pan." He carries the pan to his roommate's closed door. "Hey!" he shouts. "I told you to clean up after you cook." He hurls the frying pan against the door.

The door opens. "What the fuck's the matter with you? I just finished eating. I'll get to the pan in a minute. You don't have to throw it against my door."

An argument ensues and they go upstairs to work it out.

I leave Los Angeles. At five a.m. I say goodbye to Hervé and Suzanne. I give Hervé a book of poetry. He's touched and asks me to inscribe it. I write: "For Hervé—Deep communication our shared gem—with love and thanks, Scott."

"Think about my offer," he says as we embrace. "You could pay the same rent out here in a big country house that you pay for your small apartment in New York City."

"We'll think it over."

I take a plane from Los Angeles to Washington, D.C. where I meet Sandy. We drive to North Carolina to get additional photos of rhomboids since Death Valley didn't provide them. I tell her about my trip and about Hervé's invitation. "He's going to buy a house in the country. He wants us to live with him."

"What do you think?" Sandy asks.

"I don't know. It's certainly something to think about. Hervé feels we could break through in writing and art in L.A. more easily than in New York. He says we could pay him the same rent we're paying in Manhattan."

Sandy tempers her excitement with caution. "Herve's not the easiest person to live with. Anne's letters show that."

We arrive in Hattaras where all the rhomboids have been blurred to extinction by wind and rain in the ten days since we were last here.

We return to New York City where I begin work for the list broker. Before lunch on the first day I phone Sandy. "I'm not going to make it here. There are dozens of glass offices filled with people chain-smoking. It's like working in a polluted fish bowl."

"Try to stick with it a little longer than three hours," Sandy suggests.

"O.K., O.K.," I say, "I'll give it some time. But the place has gotten to me. We punch in and out four times a day. I feel like I'm in prison."

With each passing week of deadening work, our interest in moving to L.A. grows. Sandy writes to Hervé and asks if he's serious about sharing a house with us. We both feel that for peace of mind we need a final answer.

Six weeks pass without a response from Herve. I'm eyeing *The New York Times* "Help Wanted" section again, when a phone call at four in the morning jolts us awake.

Herve's voice sounds like he's just won the sweepstakes. "I've bought a house!" he cries. "In the country. A small ranch with two horses."

"Fantastic!" I respond.

"You and Sandy can have the upstairs. I'll have the downstairs. We can convert a barn into a studio so Sandy and I can paint. When can you move out here?"

41

"Hang on," I say. I cover the mouthpiece and feel my heart drumming wildly. "It's Hervé," I tell Sandy. "He's bought a house in the country. A small ranch with two horses. He says we can have the upstairs and he'll take the downstairs. We can convert a barn into a studio."

After a rush of excited conversation, we share the same feeling: let's do it. We hug each other for luck and I tell Hervé, "We'd love to live in the house with you. When are you moving in?"

"June 19th. You can arrive any time after that."

"Look for us toward the end of the month."

Hervé is ecstatic. And so are we. After I hang up, we dance around our apartment.

Daily work at the list broker changes for me. Several people comment on how happy I suddenly seem.

Early June—1978

Hervé calls one evening and sounds distressed. Things have gotten very heavy for him in L.A. "They've had a few kidnap threats at the studio."

"You?"

"Yeah. And every time I go out in public now I'm mobbed. It's worse than it was in Death Valley. My agent wants me to have a bodyguard—twenty-four hours a day."

I groan into the phone. "What a drag."

"It is a drag. It takes away my freedom. The bodyguard is going to live in the house with us."

"Where will he sleep?"

"Downstairs. You'll be upstairs. There are two rooms upstairs and you'll be in one. The other will be a guest room."

I discuss the changes with Sandy while Hervé holds. Though not happy with the news, we decide to go ahead

42

with the move anyway. I tell Hervé and he says, "Good. We'll go about our lives as if he's not there. And he can help us get the place into shape. There's a lot of work to do on the grounds."

"We'll be happy to chip in."

Our conversation turns upbeat. "Bring your typewriter," he says. "They're running out of ideas for 'Fantasy Island.' There's plenty of work for you out here."

This is the most encouraging news I've heard in a long time. "That's music to my ears."

Sandy talks with Hervé and asks, "What should we bring?"

"Everything," he answers. "I'm moving into a large, empty house. Bring all your furniture. I don't have anything to put in the house. My furniture is in Paris with Anne."

"Well, then maybe we won't sublet our apartment. Since you can use our stuff, it might make more sense to give up our place and move everything out."

"Yeah, good. I'll give you the address as soon as I get it."

The following day, Sandy and I give notice at our jobs.

Mid-June—1978

I phone Hervé and ask for the address. "I need it for the movers."

"Just a minute," he says. There's a long pause, followed by, "I don't want people to know where I'm living. So don't give my address out to anyone."

I jot down the address.

Sandy and I are disturbed by Herve's request not to tell anyone his new address...our new address as well. Friends and family also are disquieted.

We spend the week packing and making final arrangements. Our pitch of excitement heightens. In spite of the

43

qualifications Hervé has described, our move to L.A. still feels right to us. We're ready for a major change. We've lived in New York City on and off for eight years. It's time for something totally different. A warmer climate. Different types of people. A chance to break through professionally.

June 21, 1978

After a week of farewells to family and friends, Sandy and I watch three moving men load a van with twenty-six-hundred pounds collected over the course of our eight years together.

June 22, 1978

Our '69 Chrysler is crammed full of everything we wouldn't entrust to the movers. There's barely enough room for the two of us. With good wishes ringing in our heads, we're off, L.A. or bust.

Driving west toward the promised land, anticipation is our ally as we speed along the turnpike through Pennsylvania and Ohio.

We spend ten and twelve hours a day on the road, camping along the way, driving without sightseeing until we hit Utah. After a day in its fossilized parks and canyons, we head straight to Las Vegas, arriving late in the afternoon. We take a motel room but are so tired that after a few hours rest we're ready to get on the road again. We drive for two hours and phone Hervé.

"Where are you?"

"Your side of Las Vegas. We'll be arriving in the morning, probably around six-thirty or seven."

"If you get here before six-thirty come to the house on Normandie. If not, I'll leave a pass for you at the studio."

"See you in a few hours."

We drive through the desert beneath a sky thick with stars, our conversation rife with dreams, and arrive at Herve's house a few minutes before six-thirty. We greet each other joyfully. "You made it," he laughs, amid hugs of welcome. "I was worried about you." He gives us a detailed map showing how to get to his new house. And a key. "I'm leaving for the studio in a few minutes. After you see the house and get some sleep, drop by the set. I'll leave a pass."

Sandy and I follow his map. We travel through dry, rolling hills with power lines scarring the skyline, turn right at a horse-crossing and head down a dirt road. A cloud of dust follows us.

We pull into a horseshoe driveway and gaze at the large, two-story, tobacco-colored, wood-shingled house. Tall pine trees. A semi-circle of grass. A few scrawny shrubs. A garage at right angles with the house.

We open the front door and enter a foyer with a slate floor. A wrought iron bannister angles upstairs. A bathroom and small bedroom are off the foyer. The large living room has a high, beamed ceiling and chocolate-brown carpeting. Gray-white drapes are drawn across a picture window which runs the length of the room. We draw back the drapes and look out onto a patio and rectangular swimming pool—a touch of "Hollywood."

The living room has an impressive stone fireplace. A doorway leads to the section of the house where Hervé will live. This section consists of an office, a bedroom, bathroom and a "photo" room (where he will store his camera equipment).

There is a kitchen and dining area; the kitchen is equipped with electric burners, cabinets and drawers and is painted a sharp yellow. The ceiling is covered with bland Americana wallpaper.

45

A sliding glass door and screen door open onto steps and a dirt path. A chain-link fence separates Herve's property from a neighbor's. The path descends to the swimming pool, curves around the pool and leads to the stables. It ends at a chain-link gate. We open the gate and come upon a radically different scene: the stables and "the barn." The ambiance shifts from California country to French farmhouse. There is a dilapidated tool shed. This is the "barn" that Hervé wants to convert to a studio. We pass several empty horse stalls before coming upon a mare and her colt.

Our impression is that the place needs considerable work but has great potential. The land is an acre and a half of sloping, dry and often rocky soil, with a few eucalyptus trees. The stables are falling apart but they have graceful lines.

We return to the house. Upstairs are two rooms separated by a hallway, bathroom, and a wrought iron balcony overlooking the living room. One room is about the size of our studio apartment in New York City. It's a somber blue, clashing with the brown carpet.

"We'll have to paint this room white," Sandy says.

I agree.

The other room is about half the size, with half the closet space. We take another turn through the house and grounds, then drive to the Columbia Ranch on Oak Street near the Burbank Studios. We make our way to the "Fantasy Island" set where we find Hervé in his trailer, with an ex-girlfriend and his secretary, Linda. "Well, what do you think?" he asks.

"The place is a knockout," I say.

"It's really beautiful," Sandy adds.

He introduces us but seems strangely aloof. After a brief exchange, he says he's got a carton full of stuff from his house on Normandie Avenue. It's in Linda's car. Would we mind taking it up to the house? "I'll see you there later for dinner. You'll meet my bodyguard, Chris."

"Sounds good," Sandy says.

We follow Linda. As she hands me Hervé's carton I notice a bumper sticker on her yellow Volkswagon—"Happiness

Is Being Single." We drive off wondering why Hervé is in a dark mood. It's the first of innumerable times that we'll wonder about this.

We buy food and store it in our ice cooler. There is no refrigerator in the house yet. We pick up *TV Guide* which has a caricature of Hervé and Ricardo Montalban on the cover. The story is not entirely flattering to Herve. One sentence describes him as "pompous."

That evening we meet Hervé and Chris and have a barbeque together. Chris is fresh on the job and eager to please. About 5'6", he's in his early twenties, pleasantly handsome with a wispy moustache and ash-blonde hair. He's an advanced karate student who worked previously for James Investigation Agency. He's attentive to Hervé the way a valet is attentive to royalty.

We use paper plates and plastic forks. Hervé looks at the forks with disgust and says, "I don't want anything plastic in my house. I can't stand plastic."

I try to kid him out of it.

He repeats, "I don't want anything plastic in my house."

Chris is so anxious to make a good impression that he monopolizes conversation. It's strange for the three of us suddenly to be sharing ourselves with a bodyguard, a total stranger.

Chris cooks a steak for Hervé on an hibachi and Hervé tells him, "I like it real bloody." It's clear from the start that he resents having a 'round-the-clock bodyguard.

The following morning, the van with our twenty-six hundred pounds arrives from New York. The moving men carry everything into the larger upstairs bedroom.

When Hervé arrives he appears startled by the number of possessions we've brought with us. He motions for me to follow him. We walk into the adjacent smaller room and he says, "Don't set your things up in that room. I want to use it as a guest room. You'll be in this room."

"What's that?"

"You and Sandy can have this room."

47

I shake my head. The smaller bedroom is approximately ten by twelve. "Herve, this room is smaller than our studio apartment in New York City. We didn't drive three thousand miles and move all our stuff out here to live in a room this size. It's out of the question."

He understands from my tone of voice that it *is* out of the question. "It's too small for you?"

"Herve, there are two of us."

"O.K. You can have the other room."

Later, I tell Sandy of Herve's attempt to put us in the smaller room. We're troubled. Is this a portent of things to come?

Hervé moves in over the weekend. He has no furniture, little clothing, and few kitchen utensils. He does, however, have extensive photographic equipment and some drawings and oil paintings from his early years as an artist, as well as a collection of guns and knives.

Chris moves his belongings into the room off the foyer. He sleeps on the floor in a sleeping bag.

Our first weekend is spent in supermarkets and hardware stores. Hervé sets up a record-keeping system. On graph paper, he draws columns and writes his initials over one column, ours over another. Whatever we purchase, we write down what it is, its cost, and whether it was purchased for the house or for ourselves.

Nothing is wasted. All leftovers, eggshells, coffee grounds, etc. are deposited in a mulch pile at the stables. The fact that Hervé is now making more money in one week than he made during a year in New York or Los Angeles does not change his thrifty living habits. He clips cents-off coupons and fills a kitchen drawer with them. He tells us to check the drawer before buying any household items.

We use our gate-leg table and two Mexican chairs as a kitchen table and supplement the chairs with supermarket crates. Though the living room is empty, Hervé says he's picky about furnishings and chooses only my desk to put in it. We tell him that he can hang any of our framed original

48

lithographs but he doesn't look at them. We wonder why he asked us to bring all our stuff.

Sandy and I spend our first week waiting for plumbers, phone men, a new refrigerator; we buy supplies, line the kitchen cabinets with paper, clear the land of rocks and wood, and settle into daily chores.

Sandy feeds the cats, five of them. The two indoor cats are Hervé's. The three outdoor cats are strays that attached themselves to the house. Hervé tells Sandy that the outside cats get dry food once a day. "They should hunt mice," he says. "The indoor cats get canned food."

I water the plants, bushes and trees in front and back of the house every morning and evening, and regularly chop wood at the stables.

Hervé is pleased by the work going on. And the cause of his depression is partly revealed when he confides that his girlfriend has cut off communication without explanation. His attempts to reach her have been futile. Sandy and I listen sympathetically. We're relieved to know that something specific is causing his depression.

His mood lightens when he hires two sisters, Cindy and Diane, aged thirteen and eleven, to take care of his horses. They're lovely kids and Hervé, Sandy and I quickly form a friendship with them. They live within walking distance and feed the horses twice a day.

Unfortunately, Hervé can't ride the mare, Lucky, because her back is too broad for him to straddle. And the colt's too young to ride. Diane and Cindy tell Hervé of a pony that's for sale, and I drive them and Sandy in our car to look it over.

A young woman, perhaps seventeen, comes out, quieting two barking dogs. "You the people that called about the pony?"

Hervé nods. "Can we see it?"

"This way." She leads us to the corral, asking Hervé, "Aren't you on that TV show, 'Fantasy Island'?"

"Yeah."

49

"I *knew* I'd seen you before. My name is Debbie." She leads us into a corral to a brown and white spotted pony. "This is Lady. She's a real gentle pony. Plenty of spunk, though."

Cindy and Diane look her over carefully, examining her legs, hooves, teeth and form. "How old is she?" Cindy asks.

"Twelve."

"Is that old for a pony?" Hervé asks.

"About middle-aged," Debbie answers. "She's in real good shape for her age. You can ride her and see what I mean."

Cindy rides Lady through various paces over a hilly back yard. Dismounting, she says, "Pretty good pony," following Herve's caution not to show too much enthusiasm.

"We'd like to talk it over," Hervé says. Debbie walks away and he asks Cindy, "Well? What do you think?"

"I love her. She's easy to ride. You won't have any trouble with her."

"Is she worth $150?"

"I'd offer $125. She's got a lot of spunk for her age."

Hervé settles the deal somewhere between the two figures with a riding pad thrown in. As we leave, he spies a pile of railroad ties and asks, "Are they for sale?"

"Might be," Debbie says. "I'll ask about them and let you know."

Hervé treats us all to a Chinese lunch on the way home. He's in good spirits. He has a new passion, ponies.

When Lady is delivered, Diane and Cindy scrub her with shampoo and hose her down. They brush her coat until it dries, glistening in the sun. Hervé beams throughout the washing. He's excited about the pony and he clearly enjoys the neighborhood girls.

When they finish, Lady looks like a different pony. "She's beautiful," Cindy says. "If she lost a little weight she could be a show pony."

"A show pony?" Hervé repeats.

"Well, she could compete in her class, for sure. In fact, there's a horse show tomorrow morning."

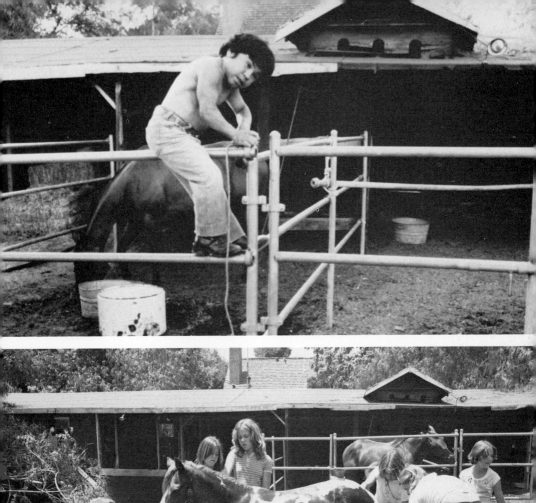

At the stables

That's all Hervé has to hear. "Let's enter her." Lady looks so beautiful that in our collective imagination we're sure she's got a good chance to place.

The following morning at seven, Cindy arrives at the stables and saddles Lady. Hervé is up and watching her. He wants to learn as much as he can about horses, as quickly as possible.

By seven-thirty, several neighborhood girls, on their horses and ponies, are waiting in the driveway for Hervé. The horses whinny and crap in turn, the sun rises, and Hervé joins the group on Lady. The entourage heads out of the driveway, Sandy and I on foot.

After an hour's trek, we arrive at the horse show: a spacious corral, a judge's stand, dozens of horse trailers, trainers with whips and crops in hand, wearing colorful cowboy shirts and stylish, skin-tight jeans and boots. All the local horse people are at the show. In Sunland, their numbers are large.

Lady is awarded a fifth prize ribbon and our contingent goes wild. On the way back, Hervé is pitched off Lady and thrown head first to the ground. This fall is the first of many. He remounts Lady with a lump on his head, his spirits undampened.

The horses and ponies are hosed down in the stables. Then the kids have cokes and we have beer. Fifth place or not, Lady won, and Hervé is whistling-happy. He places a ladder under the passageway leading to his bedroom. "As we win ribbons, we'll hang them up here," he says, smiling like the kids who affectionately watch him.

His involvement with his horses and pony and the neighborhood girls works wonders for him. He thinks about little else when he's not on the set. As soon as he returns from the Burbank Studios he goes straight to the stables and takes Lady out on the trails. Cindy and Diane usually ride with him on Lucky or one of their friend's ponies. Nothing eases Herve's frustrations like his late afternoon rides on Lady.

And nothing creates more frustration for Chris than these pony rides. Hervé tells him to stay at the house and keep in touch via walkie talkie. But Chris has been instructed by James Investigation Agency not to let Hervé out of his sight. He doesn't know what to do.

One day Hervé wants to go out on the trails alone. Chris insists on going with him. When they return, Hervé is fuming.

"What's wrong?" I ask.

"The jerk ran in front of Lady on the trail. He ruined my ride. How can you have fun when you have a bodyguard running in front of you?" Hervé grinds his teeth and says he can't stand someone shadowing him twenty-four hours a day. Later that week, he says, "Chris is making mistakes. And I don't like the way he looks at Jackie" (the Assistant Director's fourteen-year-old daughter who cleans Hervé's house on Saturdays).

"Why don't you talk to him about it?"

Hervé won't hear of it. "He's getting paid a lot of money, $20 an hour. He should know what he's doing. I shouldn't have to tell him."

"I could talk to him."

"He's the bodyguard. He should know his job."

The following day Chris mentions to Hervé that while driving his new red Porsche, he hit an owl and it broke one of his headlights.

"Do you know where you hit it?"

"Yeah."

"Go get it. I'll use the feathers to make an Indian totem. Otherwise the owl died for nothing."

Chris retrieves the wings and talons of the owl and Hervé nails them to a board and places the board on the stable roof to dry.

July 13th

Hervé's public relations agent arranges for Hervé, Sandy, Chris and me to go to a Crystal Gayle concert at The Roxy. We drive there in our Chrysler and enter quickly to avoid fans who scream, "Tattoo! Tattoo!" We're ushered to the apron of the stage and a table and four chairs are set up specially for us. Murmurs of recognition ripple through the crowded, smoky room. Photographers muscle their way toward us and flashbulbs pop.

After the show, a balding young man, notebook in hand, tells us he's from *The Hollywood Reporter*. He'd like a few photographs. He clears the area in back of him and gestures for his photographer. The four of us are photographed. Then he wants a photograph of just Sandy and Hervé.

At this moment, Crystal Gayle moves slowly through the crowd of well-wishers and spots Hervé. They met once before in Nashville. The reporter maneuvers the two of them together and they're photographed. The reporter then asks for our names, addresses, and occupations. When he asks me I tell him, "Hermann Hesse. Writer."

He scribbles and asks, "How do you spell that?"

"Two *n*'s and two *s*'s."

He writes Hermann and stops mid-Hesse. "Hey bub, I don't have time for this kind of crap. What's your name?"

"Scott Seldin. Writer."

A flashbulb showers light on Hervé and me. This photograph appears in *The Hollywood Reporter* the following day.

Hervé can't get over it. "I tried for years to get into *The Hollywood Reporter*. People pay money to get in. You're in Los Angeles two weeks and you make it. Unbelievable."

I find it more amusing than unbelievable. I spend countless

hours during the next weeks working around the house. The pile of chopped wood in front of the "barn" increases until I wonder whether it's a fire hazard.

Although much work is completed around Hervé's house, I haven't written a word since we arrived in L.A. I tell him that I'm eager to start writing. He suggests a documentary about him and discusses the possibility of turning it into a TV film. I begin work on the project that night. I make notes and hope I'll be able to depict Hervé in all his complexity: thirty-five-year-old bachelor, midget, TV star, farmer, artist, chef, gun toter; Hervé depressed, elated, impatient, funny; failures and successes; bon vivant, philosopher, business-man, purist, chauvinist, equestrian, hell raiser, dark magi-cian.

The film will explore matters of the heart and survival tactics in a basically unfriendly human environment. It will touch on the universal need for human dignity and questions rooted in what it's like to struggle in society for recognition as an artist and as a human being when you're three feet eleven inches tall.

I put the sketch in a drawer and think about the project for a few days. I begin to note a marked increase in Hervé's frustration and anxiety. He says his business manager con-trols his sizeable weekly income and most of it goes into investments and the mortgage on the house. He's given only $150 a week spending money. Even with his habitual frugality, he needs more money to run the house. Despite demands to his business manager, additional money is not forthcoming.

His irritation with Chris also increases. Finally, Chris makes a "mistake" which costs him his job. The lapse occurs during his day off. That evening, Hervé has a woman friend at the house and the four of us are having a barbeque outside. Chris appears with his girlfriend, around ten. We talk with them for a few minutes. As we move into the kitchen to clean up, Hervé watches Chris put his arms around his girlfriend's waist and head toward his bedroom.

55

"Oh no you don't," Hervé says.

Chris turns around, surprised.

"Not in my house, you don't."

It takes Chris a moment to understand and then he quickly ushers his girlfriend out of the house and drives off with her in his Porsche.

Chris is fired. Hours before the axing, Hervé tells Sandy and me of his intention. He runs through the mistakes Chris made during his two-and-a-half weeks in the house: he intruded in our conversations; he looked at Jackie the wrong way; he ran in front of him on the horse trail ruining his ride; he ordered the most expensive food in restaurants; he tried to stay overnight with his girlfriend.

These reasons don't seem compelling to us but Hervé has made up his mind. We're in the kitchen when Chris walks in singing a jaunty rendition of "Get A Job." The irony is painful.

Hervé acts with explosive swiftness. He phones his agent, Arnold, from the kitchen, with Chris on the steps outside the screen door.

"I want Chris out of here today," he says gruffly. "I've had it with him." After a brief conversation, he hangs up and waits near the phone. Arnold calls James Investigation Agency. Minutes later, the phone rings and Hervé picks it up.

"That's right," he says firmly. "I want him out today. Hang on, I'll get him. Chris," he calls. "It's for you."

Chris saunters into the kitchen, says "Hello" into the phone and his face blanches.

Hervé disappears into his room. Chris hangs up and turns toward us, bewildered. "I've been fired."

"We're really sorry, Chris," Sandy says. "Hervé told us earlier this morning that he was going to do this."

"Did he say why?"

"He mentioned a few things, nothing important."

"Like what?" He shakes his head.

A few hours later, Chris is gone. His swift departure is

unnerving. We fill in as bodyguard and companion during the following evenings and weekend. And we paint our room, as much to escape the tension in the house as to establish that this is indeed our room.

When we finish, we call Hervé to take a look. He points to our chest of drawers near the doorway. "It doesn't look good here. It should go over there." He inspects the paint job and concludes, "The molding should be a darker white to set it off."

"Hervé, the chest doesn't fit over there. And we like the trim as it is."

He leaves and we're left standing in the room, wondering how long we'll live in it.

One day Hervé invites a writer/director friend, Alan Glickman, over for lunch. He also invites a writer, ex-girlfriend, Nancy. Hervé calls, "Sandy, we're having a few friends over for lunch. Will you make a salad?"

Sandy senses the assumed role of "cook" implicit in his voice. She and I prepare a salad. At lunch, Alan announces that he has a producer for a documentary about Hervé which he's going to write and direct.

My jaw drops, and Hervé picks up on my reaction.

"Scott is a writer," he says, "and I told him he could write a documentary about me. Sandy is an artist and she's going to work on it too."

Alan describes the new TV series "Comeback" for which he's writing the documentary. It will be aired for the first time next winter and they've got top names as subjects for the show.

"Speak to my agent about it," Hervé tells him.

That afternoon I take Hervé aside and say, "I'm still going to write the documentary, aren't I?"

"You can write it and Alan can direct it."

Around five, I remind Hervé about dinner at my aunt and uncle's at seven-thirty. Several times during the week I checked with him to be sure he was free.

But he's got his eye on Nancy. He turns to me and says,

57

"I'm not going to be able to make it. I'd just fall asleep at the table." With a rueful grin, he adds, "Around here, we do whatever we want. Can you two stay for dinner?"

They have other appointments.

"Break them," he says.

Nancy wavers but Alan says, "I never break appointments."

Hervé convinces Nancy to stay for dinner. I call my uncle, telling him that Hervé won't be able to make it. Sandy and I go to dinner and return around ten. As we walk into the kitchen, Hervé comments, "Back so soon?"

The following day we're subdued. But Hervé is animated and affectionate around us. He tells us he's going to be on the "Tomorrow" show and "The Merv Griffin Show," back to back. He'd like us to be with him at the tapings. We tell him we'd like to go.

Late afternoon on the taping day, Maribeth and Hervé pull into the driveway. She's filling in as bodyguard. Hervé hurries into the house.

"Guess where we've been?" Maribeth says with a grin.

"Where?" Sandy asks.

"A hardware store. I couldn't pull him out of there. I told him, 'Hervé, you're going to be late for the show,' but oh no, he had to look at one more thing."

Hervé whips out the front door and trots toward us, bare-chested and barefoot. He's carrying clothing and a pair of cowboy boots.

We speed toward the NBC Studio in Burbank for the "Tomorrow" show. On the way, Hervé dons a cowboy shirt, a red bandanna, socks and boots. He appears exceptionally relaxed and in good humor.

We're shown to the Green Room and he's led away for makeup. We're offered drinks and the TV, hanging mid-wall like an appendage, is turned on. Hervé enters, made up, and anxious to get on with it. He follows Elia Kazan. To the probing questions about his background, Hervé talks dramatically, and somberly, about his early days in New York

City, learning how to survive street violence while holed up in his hotel room, learning English from TV westerns.

After the show, Hervé, Sandy and I are driven to "The Merv Griffin Show." The car stops at the back entrance and a crowd spots Hervé as he steps out of the car. I run interference amid the flashbulbs and shouts of "Tattoo!" Inside, we're offered drinks by a solicitous bartender. The room fills with show biz people and their guests. A large TV, also anchored mid-wall, is turned on. Everyone in the room roots for special guests as Merv Griffin introduces them.

Hervé is given a laudatory "hot property" introduction by Merv and the audience receives him enthusiastically with prolonged applause. He acknowledges the applause with charm and affection and eases effortlessly into conversation. Merv comments on his cowboy outfit, his success co-starring on "Fantasy Island," and the ranch he's just bought in the Los Angeles area.

"You live in that big house all by yourself?"

"No," Hervé answers. "I live there with my best friend, Scott, who is a writer, and his wife, Sandy, who is an artist." He talks about his horses, plans for his "small ranch," and the neighborhood girls who feed his horses and ride with him.

After the show, Hervé takes everyone to dinner. He's in an expansive, warmhearted mood. We return to the house and the feeling of tight friendship and accessibility continues through the days which follow.

Jim Campbell, head of James Investigation Agency, and Maribeth, show up during the week with full-time bodyguard number two. We're introduced to Cal, over six feet, thin, not particularly muscular, an expert in one of the martial arts, a soft-spoken young man in his early twenties.

Cal gets the job. Shortly after he moves into the house, I take him aside. "I'd like to fill you in on what the last bodyguard did wrong."

"I'd really appreciate that."

None of us wants a repeat firing. I advise Cal to be by

59

himself when he's in the house. He's responsible for his own food and he's to clean up immediately after eating. He's not to walk into Hervé's room unannounced and there's no reason for him to be upstairs. He's to be as invisible as possible.

Cal thanks me and says, "It's difficult to enter a situation like this where three people have known each other for eight years and suddenly I'm here, a fourth roommate."

"You're definitely *not* a fourth roommate. You've been hired as a bodyguard. You work for Hervé. We don't. We pay rent here."

Cal says he understands and our first week together works out well. He spends hours with us, shovelling manure, sawing wood, cleaning the swimming pool; after dinner he leaves the three of us alone so we can talk in privacy. But this harmony doesn't last long.

Hervé gets a phone call one morning from two sisters, fifteen and thirteen years old, runaways, stranded without money, somewhere in Florida. He tells them he'll wire money for bus fare but they'll have to pay him back. They can stay with him while they work off their debt. He relates this phone conversation to me.

"How long will they be staying?"

"As long as it takes for them to work off their debt."

"When do they arrive?"

"In about a week." Then smiling, "I really love those girls. I met them on Venice Beach last spring. Venice is a rough area. They were panhandlers. I told them I wouldn't give them money but I'd buy them a meal. I found out they lived on the beach and hooked when they needed money. They told me stories about their lives, about everyone ripping everyone off; they didn't trust anyone. I wanted to show them they could trust me. They stayed at my house on Normandie Avenue. We slept in the same bed and I never touched them. I wanted them to know they could trust me."

I'm not supportive of his plan. I tell Sandy about the latest shifting of household sands. She feels as I do. All the newspapers and magazines need is to get wind that two runaway sisters, fifteen and thirteen, live with Hervé Villechaize, co-star of "Fantasy Island."

The more we think about his plan the less comfortable we feel about it. We're the ones who will have responsibility for the sisters while he's off at the studio. Finally, I ask him, "Hervé, these two sisters live in Venice, right?"

"That's right."

"How far away is that?"

"About an hour."

"Well, I'd be happy to pick them up at the beach every morning and take them home in the evening. I don't think it's a good idea to have them stay in the house overnight."

Hervé tightens. "Why not?"

"Because they're underage. You'd be crazy to risk your career. I'll pick them up every morning and take them home every night."

"No. They're going to live here. I told them they could stay."

"Does Arnold know about this?"

"Arnold doesn't have to know everything I do."

"You respect him, right?"

"So?"

"So get his opinion. He has a right to know. Your body-guard protects you from physical danger. Arnold takes care of dangers to your career."

Hervé resists. "People are afraid to act like this. They only want to be around 'good' people. They don't want to take chances. I love those girls. I want to take a chance with them. Where would I be if people didn't take a chance with me? I know I might get ripped off. I always figure there's a 50-50 chance I'm going to get ripped off whenever I do anything."

The matter rides until the end of the month, when an incident occurs that finally ruptures emotions.

At breakfast, Cal tells me, "You and Sandy slept through everything last night."

"Slept through what?"

"The police. They rang the bell around two in the morning. I was half asleep. I said, 'I just started work here. I'm a bodyguard.' They said they had a report of a burglary. I told them there'd been no burglary here and they left. About an hour later, they came back. They said again, 'We have a report of a burglary. Can we come in?'"

"This happened last night?"

"Yeah. So they come in and split up. One of them heads straight for Hervé's room. I follow him and he shines a big flashlight in Hervé's eyes. Hervé reaches for his .22. The policeman grabs the .22 and empties the bullets into his hand. Hervé tells him he wants his gun back. They go into the living room to talk things over. The other policeman is waiting there. They say they had a burglary report. Hervé tells them there's been no burglary here. The policeman returns his rifle and they leave."

I sip my espresso. "This all happened last night?"

"Around two or three in the morning."

"Smells like a set-up to me."

"Uh huh."

"You let the cops in?"

"Sure."

"Why?"

"I wanted to clear the situation up."

I shake my head. "Cal, you're the bodyguard. You're supposed to keep strangers out. You get paid to do that."

"I know, but they were policemen."

"So you let them in."

"Yeah."

"What was the first thing the cops said when they came into the house, the exact words?"

He half-closes his eyes. "One of them said, 'Are there any young girls living here?'"

I lean forward on my seat. "Are there any young girls living here?"

"That's right."

"We *are* being set up. What did you tell him?"

62

"I said, 'No.'"

"And?"

"He pointed upstairs and asked, 'Who lives up there?' I said 'Scott and Sandy Seldin.' He asked, 'How old are they?' I said, 'Thirty-three and thirty-one.' Then the other policeman headed for Hervé's room and I followed him in."

Hervé comes in for coffee and joins in the telling. "Someone could have been shot," he says. He turns toward Cal. "You shouldn't have let the cops in."

"I wanted to clear the matter up."

"How did you know they were really cops?" I ask. "They could have been anyone dressed in cop uniforms."

"A police car was in the driveway."

Suddenly I recall something that happened while Chris was still bodyguard. Karen, a fourteen-year old, was riding Hervé's horse, Lucky. The horse reared and fell over backwards on top of her. She was knocked out briefly and managed, with Cindy's help, to make her way to Hervé's house. Hervé was alone at the time. Cindy phoned the local paramedics and Hervé brought Karen into his bedroom to examine her for broken bones. When the paramedics arrived they found Hervé checking Karen all over for injuries.

I also recall an incident that occurred the following afternoon. I answered the doorbell. Two cops were standing there. One asked if this was 10340 Wheatland. I told him, no, wrong address. They returned to their police car. I ask Cal, "Did one of the cops last night have a moustache? Was he swarthy with a moustache?"

"Yeah, one of them was like that."

"Does the paramedic's report go to the local cops?"

The general opinion is that it does. The connection between the paramedics and the cops makes sudden sense.

"These are local cops," I remark. "They should know the difference between local street addresses."

Hervé agrees. "Who can be setting me up? Not many people know I live here." He counts the number and comes up with nine or ten. "It could be Chris. He's got reason to

63

want to get back at me. Who else? Maybe my ex-girlfriend Ginger's mother? No, I don't think so."

Arnold and Jim Campbell are phoned and told details of the pre-dawn incident. Jim says he'll investigate right away. In the flurry of subsequent phone calls, Jim and Arnold learn of Hervé's plan to have the two runaway sisters stay with him at the house. Arnold hits the roof. And Jim says, "If the girls move in I'll pull my man out of the house."

Paranoia sparks numerous conversations during the next few days. One such conversation ends late at night with tears running down Hervé's face; another ends with Hervé and me after midnight at a tense impasse.

"I love those girls," he argues. "I want to help them. If I don't help them, who will?"

"You don't have to do something that's going to risk your career. That's what you're doing, you know. Ask Roman Polanski."

His hands curl into fists. "I don't care about my career. I can't live like this. I don't want a house if I can't have anyone I want stay in it."

"You're ready to give up your career over this?"

"Yes."

"O.K. Chucking everything *is* an alternative. But tell me something. Would you be so eager to help these two run-aways if they were two young teenage boys instead of two young teenage girls?"

He doesn't answer. Finally he says, "That's a good question. I think I would help them if they were runaway boys." He grows morose. "I don't want to live in this country with its stupid laws. I'll leave. I don't need this house. I don't need anything. If they want to set me up, let them do it. I don't care. If it's not these girls it will be someone else. It could be an addict. It could be someone who just got out of jail."

The following evening Hervé rides off on his pony alone. All of us anxiously await his return. Several hours later we hear pistol shots. Hervé walks up to the house from the stables, flashlight in one hand, pistol in the other. He tells us, "I shot another black widow near the swimming pool."

Hervé's lawyer advises him that the only legal way to have the girls live with him is to have a policewoman also living in the house with them. This alternative is too complicated so when the sisters call from L.A., Hervé tells them they won't be able to stay at his house. He invites them to visit, telling them his bodyguard will pick them up.

But Cal is fired before this can happen. His firing is different from Chris'. Sandy and I return to the house after a few morning errands. Hervé meets us as our car pulls up, and says, "There's a revolution going on in the house. I asked Cal to make coffee for me and he replied, 'Make it yourself. I'm not your boy. I was hired as bodyguard and I'm not going to work around the house anymore.'"

Within seconds, Hervé is on the phone, talking with Arnold. He cites the insubordination and says, "I want him out today." Ten minutes later the phone rings. Cal is told by Jim Campbell that he's been fired and to clear out immediately.

"Sorry it had to end like this," Cal says to Sandy, Linda and me. "Another time, another place, who knows? We might have been friends."

He returns an hour later to pick up his bicycle. He rings the doorbell to alert us, saying he doesn't want to be shot by mistake. I help put his bicycle into the car and ask, "Why'd you blow the job over a pot of coffee?"

"It wasn't just the coffee," he explains. "It was Hervé's attitude. I don't like being ordered around like a slave. Do this, do that. You're a writer, huh? Well, I don't know how you can work in an atmosphere like this."

We're back to square one. Maribeth fills in as bodyguard and Hervé decides he doesn't want a sleep-in replacement for Cal. Maribeth takes the job full-time during weekdays. And the pilot for James Investigation Agency, Dave, takes the weekend shift. Dave is in his thirties, with no experience in the martial arts, a slight paunch, and a cleanliness fetish.

Hervé doesn't ask him to work on the grounds with us, saying "He's too clean."

One of Dave's first instructions is to pick up the two sisters from Venice Beach. They arrive with a seen-too-much-of-the-world look. After spending the afternoon eating potato chips and drinking cokes, Hervé asks if they want to go swimming.

"Can I swim nude?"

Hervé shakes his head.

"Why? There ain't no perverts around."

"The neighbors wouldn't understand."

The girls swim in make-shift suits. Before they're driven back to Venice, Hervé asks if they're still living on the beach.

"Naw," the older sister says. "We're staying with my boyfriend."

"How old is he?"

"Thirty-four."

"Why do you go out with an older guy like that?"

The girls laugh and one says, "When you go out with a sixteen-year old all he wants is to get into your pants. A thirty-four-year old is interested in something else too."

Later, Hervé bitterly says, "What good is my life if I can't help people? If I don't take a chance with them, who will? If people didn't take a chance with me I wouldn't be alive today."

He buys another pony. And the neighborhood girls play an increasingly important role in his life. "I live for those girls," he tells us frequently. "They're the only meaning in my life."

That week I receive an emergency phone call from Maribeth. She's at St. Joseph's Hospital. She was driving with Hervé, Cindy and Diane when Hervé suddenly clutched his stomach and couldn't breathe. "They gave him a shot of something. He's feeling a little better now."

"I'll be right there," I tell her. Half an hour later I walk into the hospital, and spot Maribeth.

"How is he?"

66

"Better," she says. "But there's some girlfriend with him and she's bombed out of her mind. She won't leave him alone. She's slobbering all over him."

"Who is she?"

"I don't know. Name is Julie. He had a date with her tonight. Asked me to phone and tell her he was in the hospital and couldn't make it. She arrived barely able to walk."

"What happened to Cindy and Diane?"

"Their mom came for them."

"Where's Hervé?"

"Straight through that door. I tell you, it was bad. He thought he was going under. He was fighting with them. He didn't want to be put out. He thought he'd never wake up."

"We've got to get Julie out of there."

"Absolutely. She's all over him, smothering him with wet kisses."

I walk to Hervé's curtained cubicle. Julie, in a tight black dress, has Hervé's face buried in her breasts. He's having difficulty breathing.

I return to Maribeth. We decide to ask a nurse to get Julie out.

I go back to Hervé. "How you doing?"

"Better," he says, weakly.

"Couldn't breathe?"

He shakes his head. "Same thing happened when I visited you and Sandy in Woodstock."

"Suffern. Yeah, I remember. You scared the shit out of me."

A nurse draws the curtain to one side and says, "Sorry, there are too many people in here."

Julie lifts into a theatrical pose and says, "I must stay."

She's smashed. She looks at me and repeats in a stage whisper, "I must stay with Hervé."

Maribeth phones Arnold and he says he'll be right over. His concern for Hervé extends well beyond an agent-actor relationship.

Maribeth finally cajoles Julie out of the cubicle. Julie steps into the waiting room and lights a cigarillo. I point to the No Smoking sign.

"Can't smoke in here either," she mumbles. "May as well go home."

"Hervé's going to be fine. He just needs rest. Give me your number and I'll call you later and tell you how he's doing."

"You mean I can't go with him now to the house?"

"No. He needs to sleep. The doctor said he needs complete rest, no visitors for a while."

She pouts and scribbles her number on a piece of paper. "Call me, huh? Let me know how he is. Promise you'll call."

"I promise."

She leaves and I return to Hervé. The nurse asks, "Will you help him on with his clothes?"

I nod and she and Maribeth leave. "Come on," I say, "let's get your clothes on." He's groggy and quite out of it.

A few minutes later the nurse calls, "All dressed in there?"

"All dressed," I reply. She enters, pushing a wheel chair. We help him into the chair and he's wheeled into the lobby. He signs a release and is rolled to Maribeth's car.

Arnold arrives twenty minutes later. I've been waiting for him before returning to Sunland. He rushes up to me and asks, "How is he?"

I reply, "He's gone."

All blood drains from Arnold's face. "He's...gone?"

"Yeah. Maribeth drove him home about twenty minutes ago."

He sighs audibly. "Whew! He's O.K.?"

"Sure."

"Thanks a lot, Scott." We shake hands, he walks to his white Mercedes and drives off. I drive to Sunland and find Hervé asleep in his room.

"How is he?" I ask Sandy.

"I made some food for him," she says. "He was starving. I hope he's sleeping now."

68

Hervé sleeps intermittently through the evening. I call Julie and tell her he's feeling better.

"Tell him I send my love, O.K.?"

"O.K."

When I next check on him he's sitting up in bed, an Indian blanket pulled to his chest, a floor fan circulating the air. I tell him, "I just spoke with Julie. She sends her love."

"Julie?" he says, clearing his mind. "Oh yeah, Julie. Hey, I have a date with her tonight."

"Don't you remember Julie at the hospital? She was all over you."

"Sort of."

"You couldn't breathe and she couldn't get enough of you. Remember?"

"Not really."

I fill him in and he smiles at the thought of her. "She's too much. She always causes a scene. She doesn't care where she is. Remember when you were in L.A. last winter? We had lunch with Arnold and he told me not to hang around with people who caused scenes. Remember?"

"Yeah."

"He was talking about Julie. I had a big scene in a restaurant with her and it got back to Arnold."

We leave him alone so he can sleep and he doesn't awaken until late the following morning. He walks into the kitchen, restless, and putters about, organizing hardware and tools on the floor. Illness is an annoyance to him. He views it as valuable time lost forever. He recuperates quickly; as in the past, he awakens each morning with nose-bleeds, stomach cramps and/or headaches. The only medicine that helps him is a "French" remedy which he mixes himself. His physical well-being seems subject to the same extreme ups and downs as his moods.

A few days later, he's riding his pony again. He shows me an issue of *Photoplay* which contains an interview with him. One section reads: "My business manager has put me

69

on an allowance because I'm a bit too philanthropic with my money. I'm always giving it away.

"I help people, but I cannot help the world. I try not to give money away, but if a friend of mine needs something, I buy it for him. I must tell you that I do not see any sense in making money, of being on television, if I cannot help people with my money. I wouldn't be doing it unless I could make others happy."

He tells us that "Fantasy Island" is going to film stock shots in Hawaii. He'll be there a week or more and wants us to go with him. He'll work out the details, maybe get the studio to pay for most of it. He'll tell them he needs us along as his psychiatrists, or maybe his photographers. "No," he decides, "I'll tell them you're going as my bodyguard. It will be cheaper for me to take both of you than to pay for a bodyguard."

He's starting to flex his muscle as co-star of a hit TV show. He talks to Arnold about taking us with him to Hawaii and the studio brass agree to pick up the hotel tab for Sandy and me on the island of Kauai where they'll be filming.

"We're going to Mauii first," he tells us. "For just a few days. Maybe they'll pick up the hotel bill for that too."

Sandy and I have mixed feelings. We have only a few thousand dollars left. We discuss whether we should be spending our time looking for work. I decide to write a "treatment" for "Fantasy Island" to get things rolling in that direction. But Hawaii is too enticing to pass up.

I spend the following days working around the house and writing a treatment. At last, the original vision we all had for living together in the house prevails. The three of us get together each night after dinner and, over a bottle of wine, discuss a film about horses that Hervé wants to make with us. He's thinking in terms of a documentary and suggests we shoot Super 8 film of the next horse show to interest a producer in our project. Creative juices flow. I suggest a fictional plot for the movie, based on Hervé's desire to star in the film.

Hervé and Sandy like the plot. Hervé buys a pack of

70

Expressing himself

twenty-four Super 8 cartridges with our August rent money and we shoot a few practice rolls at the stables. We take his equipment and ponies to the next local horse show and film the event. Dave, the weekend bodyguard, accompanies us. And "Whiskey," Hervé's most recently purchased pony, wins fourth prize.

Hervé accepts the ribbon, the judges congratulate him, and one of them asks, "Did you see the miniature stallion that's for sale?"

"Oh no," Hervé says, grinning, and covering his eyes in mock desperation. "I can't buy any more horses. I can't afford it."

"Take a look at him. He's a beauty and he's going for only a hundred dollars."

Hervé's interest perks. "A hundred dollars?" He takes a look at the miniature stallion and falls in love, sighing, "Beautiful conformation." He examines the horse, pats its nose, and asks Cindy her opinion. She says he's worth the hundred dollars.

Hervé borrows the money from Dave and buys the horse. We ride home with "Sparky" in tow and Hervé delighted with his fourth-place ribbon. By the time we reach the house he's talking about importing a pure white horse from the Camargue in southern France, so he can win first prize. He hangs the fourth-place ribbon next to the fifth-place ribbon.

A few days later, the house is invaded when Alan Glickman directs the documentary he has written of Hervé's life for the show "Comeback." The morning of the filming, I hear Hervé downstairs. I find him puttering with his tools on the kitchen floor.

"Hi."

"Morning."

"Want some coffee?"

His eyes light up.

I prepare a pot of espresso and the doorbell rings. I open the door and a young blonde woman says, "I'm from makeup."

"Come in. Want some coffee?"

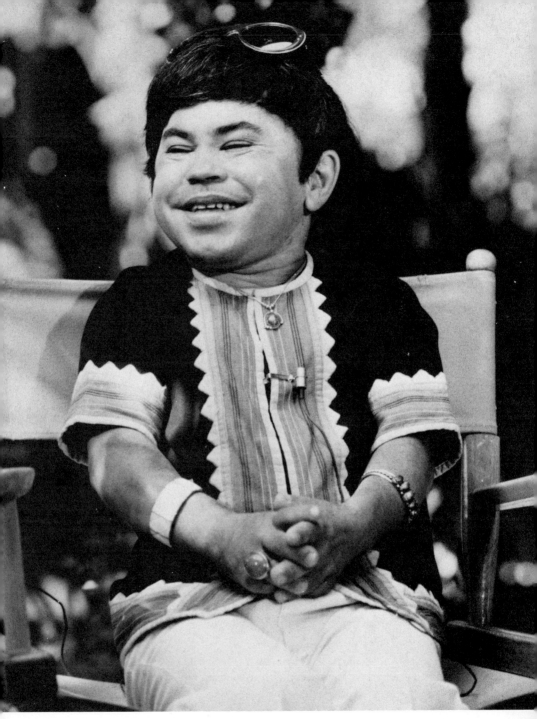

A private joke

"Sure." She introduces herself and sets her makeup case on the floor.

After some small talk the woman confides that she's working non-union. "I could get into the union by sleeping with the right people. But I don't want to do it that way."

Hervé sits with early morning sunlight on his face while the makeup artist plies her trade.

Cars, stationwagons and vans pull into the driveway. Camera equipment and lights are hauled into the living room. I help orient people to the house and grounds.

Alan Glickman paces about, giving instructions to the cameraman, the lighting man, and the production crew.

Hervé, who has not painted in years, sets up his easel, paints and palette in front of the fireplace. Alan positions lights around him and shoots the first of many takes. Hervé paints a large canvas and talks about what life was like when he lived in a seedy midtown hotel in Manhattan, surrounded by street violence.

His recitation differs from the early Manhattan experiences Alan had written into the script. He asks Hervé to repeat what he said when interviewed. Hervé explains he can't repeat it exactly: every time he tells a story it will be different.

Alan directs several more takes. He's not satisfied. "You're too stiff," he tells Hervé, who stiffens more.

Alan soothes, "Try to be the way you were when I interviewed you. You were much looser then."

"It's hard to talk like this to no one," Hervé retorts. "It sounds too much like a speech."

I spend the morning brewing espresso, getting props from Hervé's camera room, and trying to maintain a semblance of order in the kitchen, which comes under periodic siege by hungry crew members.

Around noon, a half-dozen kids arrive with a woman. I've never seen her or the kids. One of the producers escorts the kids to the hammock near the pool. The woman joins the proceedings inside. The kids giggle loudly.

74

Preparing for the documentary "Comeback"

I go outside and tell them to quiet down. We can hear them in the living room. They press the backs of their hands against their mouths, but they can't stop giggling.

Alan is finally satisfied. "O.K." he says, "we're running a little late. Can we set up outside in the driveway, please?"

The equipment is broken down and Hervé mutters to me, "I told Alan not to bring those kids. If he needed kids I have plenty in the neighborhood." He disappears into his room. When he returns, he's wearing a tee shirt with the word GROW lettered across the front.

He's filmed walking with the kids, wheeling his bicycle, dribbling a basketball. The cameraman sits in a wheel chair and tracks the group as it approaches him.

Hervé relates to the kids easily and naturally. Consequently, it takes less time to get a good take. He suggests they move the equipment to the stables and shoot the next segment of him feeding the horses because the horses haven't been fed and it's after one in the afternoon.

Alan wants to break for lunch first. Hervé insists they shoot the stable scenes first. Alan walks to the kitchen. "Break for lunch," he says and there's a rush toward the cartons of submarine sandwiches.

An angry Hervé responds, "My animals come first." He stays angry for the rest of the day.

After lunch, a few neighborhood kids and Hervé saddle horses and ponies and gallop up the road. Then they gallop back to the stables past whirring cameras.

One of the producers approaches me. "I saw you taking pictures of Hervé. How would you like to earn a quick $25?"

"Sure. What do I have to do?"

"Take a cast picture and a few shots of everyone around the stables. I'll pay for processing."

I hop to my first opportunity to earn money in L.A.; I take a few action shots of Hervé and a group cast shot. The producer scribbles his address and hands it to me.

I impulsively say, "By the way, I'm a writer as well as a photographer. If you're looking for a good writer, give me a call." I'm surprised by my boldness.

He steps back and with mock admiration says, "No—a writer too? Why, that's terrific. Maybe you'd like to write one of our scripts. It would be a quick $750. You could knock it out on a weekend. I'll give you a call if an appropriate script idea comes along."

"Great," I mumble. "I'd appreciate that."

Finally the last crew member leaves. The house is a shambles. The living room carpet is scarred by cigarette ashes and burns. The kitchen is littered with overflowing garbage bags and buzzing with hundreds of flies zigzagging between the kitchen and the living room.

Sandy and I use rolled newspapers to do battle with the flies. The place feels violated. The following morning, we spend hours carting out garbage, vacuuming, washing the kitchen floor and killing flies. The filming of Alan's documentary points up the disturbing fact that most of my time has been spent getting Hervé's house and grounds into shape. Our money is dwindling and the chill hand of necessity rests on my shoulder. I decide to get my first "Fantasy Island" treatment into the producer's hands before we leave for Hawaii. I also decide to seek work as an extra on the set. Hervé has told me that if I want work as an extra to talk to a man named Rick.

I drive to the Burbank Studios and find the crew of the documentary "Comeback" filming Hervé between "Fantasy Island" takes. Hervé is in an uncooperative mood. Alan dogs his steps and interviews him, persisting in the face of Hervé's clipped responses.

"Fantasy Island" breaks for lunch. Alan wants one more take of Hervé talking about his struggles. Hervé is openly annoyed with Alan by this time. In fact, they're barely on speaking terms. Alan films a final take of Hervé recounting his struggles and they call it a wrap. He bends low to hug Hervé goodbye but Hervé shies away.

I talk to Rick who heads Extras. He knows that I live with Hervé. He puts an arm around my shoulder. "You want to be an extra? Sure, get Hervé to write a letter to the producer saying he wants you as an extra. You pay your four hundred and something dollars and become union and you're in. How old are you?"

"Thirty-three."

"You could pass for twenty-six. Tell them you're twenty-six. You'll get called more." He looks me over. "I suppose you know how extras are generally treated on a set, herded from one place to another, like cattle. You have to decide whether that's for you. I think you should know what you're getting yourself into before you put down your money. Extras are second-class citizens."

My desire to work as an extra disappears. "Thanks for the straight information," I tell him.

It's clear by now that "Fantasy Island" isn't running out of ideas, nor writers to turn out the popular fantasies, and the problem of maintaining Hervé's well-being is unrelenting. He's accident prone.

One afternoon he returns from a pony and horseback ride with a friend of his from New York named Mary. His head is throbbing from a fall he's taken while racing on a trail.

"This fall was worse than the last," he says, a touch of pride in his voice. He needs a drink so they go to a Mexican restaurant. Maribeth and I join them.

The restaurant has two heavy wooden front doors. As I open the entrance door, the adjacent exit door swings open and its heavy metal handle smashes into Hervé's head, sending him reeling backwards. We grab him and steady him; he holds his head in his hands in pain and almost passes out. The woman who opened the exit door apologizes profusely, saying she didn't see him. A small cut is opened on his forehead and a large lump is forming. He tells the woman it's O.K. He's groggy and disoriented. We ask if he wants to go to a hospital for X-rays and he says no. He orders a double margarita to numb the pain.

We're worried about his condition. "The drink should be on the house," Hervé tells the waiter, half kidding.

Over his mild objections, we drive him to the hospital for X-rays. They're negative.

Maribeth is shaken by her inability to prevent the accident. We assure her that it wasn't anyone's fault.

A nurse gives Hervé a prescription and he comes on to her, saying, "I know the best medicine. How about coming home with me?" As we leave, he tells me, "Nurses really like to fuck."

In the following days, our thoughts turn to Hawaii. And Anne. Hervé has been in frequent phone communication with her, has asked her to come with us to Hawaii, and later live with us in Sunland. They've been apart three years. He's spent thousands of dollars talking with her by phone, trying to "get her back." She's resisted. She doesn't want to get involved with him again. But she's fallen on hard times: she's split with her lover and she owes money. Hervé finally convinces her to join us, arguing that she can always return to her job and apartment in Paris. He says he'll pay all her debts and she can owe him "one big debt."

When Anne says "yes," the mood in the house turns euphoric. We all but dance on the tables. She's scheduled to arrive in L.A. the day before we leave for Hawaii.

Sandy and Jackie clean and arrange the guest room upstairs after Hervé decides it will be Anne's room. He makes it clear that while he's excited about her coming, he wants to keep his freedom to sleep with other women. They're not going to be "married" again. His remarks about her swing from, "I really think she's the one for me," to, "When Anne gets here she's going to have to do anything I want." He tells us, "You won't believe how much she's changed. She's not the same Anne she was when we lived in Soho. After three years on her own in Paris she's much harder."

We shrug off his words and prepare for the trip to Hawaii. We set aside five hundred dollars for the fiftieth state from our shrinking reserve of money.

One evening, I tell Hervé, "I have to start making money as a writer when we get back from Hawaii."

He responds warmly. "Write a story about me. You won't have any trouble selling it. You don't even have to interview

79

me. You know who I am. You know how I live and what I do around here. Write what you want."

"Thanks very much. That's a great idea."

Later he tells us, "You know, I don't want you to pay rent any more. The $280 doesn't mean much to me. The house is paid for every month whether you pay me or not. You shouldn't have to worry about getting the money together each month. There's plenty of work to do around here."

We tell him we prefer to pay rent. He turns toward Sandy and affectionately throws an arm around her shoulder. "Sandy, tell him he's being a jerk. He should spend his time writing. And you should be painting."

"I'd like to be painting," Sandy says. "I hope we can start building the studio soon."

"Really, you don't have to pay rent. There's plenty of work to do around the place."

"No," Sandy says. "The agreement was that we'd pay the same rent we paid in New York: $280. It was fair then and it's fair now."

"The house is paid for whether you pay me or not."

"Thanks," I say, "but we want to stick with the original deal."

"That's what I tell everyone. I don't tell them you pay rent. I tell them we have a deal."

"You do?"

"That's what I told my business manager. He gives me only $150 a week. I'm trying to get more money from him and if I tell him you're paying rent he won't give me any more."

He finally drops the subject of rent. Work continues around the house.

I consider the story I'll write about Hervé. He's been interviewed by scores of newspaper and magazine writers. But the complexity of his character has not yet been conveyed. I think how true the saying is that you never really know someone until you live together.

Hervé spends his spare time before Hawaii working with

Co-stars

Miguel, a Mexican jack-of-all trades, who is building a rabbit hutch, following Hervé's design. Miguel boasts he can do anything from construction to breeding horses. Hervé spends $400 in materials before concluding that Miguel has his limitations.

Hervé talks to us about firing Miguel and getting a Mexican couple to live in a shack on the property. "I could pay them $2.50 an hour and they'd be happy. They could take care of the work around here, like caretakers."

"Living in a shack?" Sandy asks.

"Why not?"

"Sounds like a bad idea to me," I say. "With the four of us living here we should be able to do most of the chores ourselves and you could hire someone to do the heavy work."

Hervé picks up on this. "I figure if we do everything ourselves we'll each have to work twenty-one hours a week. That's with the four of us working."

"We can talk about it when Anne comes and we return from Hawaii," Sandy says.

He nods in agreement.

Hawaii is only a few days away. I complete a treatment for "Fantasy Island" and show it to Hervé. He particularly likes the part I've written for him. He's complained since we arrived in L.A. about the childish, stupid parts written for him. "They have me stand around and say 'Yes, Boss' to Ricardo all the time." He says he'll take my treatment to the producer personally. "Of course," he adds, "I'll take 10% of what they pay you if they accept it." He grins. "I'm Jewish when it comes to business."

I wince.

He adds, "Friendship is friendship and business is business."

When he returns that evening he tells me, "I read your treatment to everyone in the trailer before I took it to the producer. They said it's better than any of the scripts they've seen."

82

Between takes at Malibu

Later, the three of us sit on the living room floor and watch Hervé on "The Merv Griffin Show," taped five weeks earlier. He talks about his house and says, "I live there with my best friend, Scott, who is a writer, and his wife Sandy, who is an artist." After the words are spoken on TV, he puts an arm around each of us and says, "Did you hear that? My best friends."

The following evening he shakes my hand and says, "Congratulations. You've got yourself an agent."

"I do?"

"Arnold. I showed him the proof sheets of your interview photographs of me and he liked them. From now on we're not going to have photographers come to the house from outside to photograph me. You can be the photographer. My P.R. people need stock shots of me around the house, with my animals, that sort of stuff. I told them I have a good photographer living in my house. When we get back from Hawaii you have the job."

"Fantastico." Things are finally breaking our way.

He continues: "When I told Arnold I took your treatment to the producer myself he told me not to do it again. He doesn't want me involved with the producer that way. He said he'll make sure your treatments are read by them."

We tend to final details. A friend of Hervé's agrees to house-sit while we're away. Her name is Dena and she stops over one evening for instructions. She's tall and rangy and uninhibited the way Janis Joplin was uninhibited. She's a "Studio" singer and she projects her normal speaking voice in a loud, hyper, post-three-cups-of-coffee manner. She tells us she's just cut a demo record and asks if we'd like to hear it. She plays the cassette on our tape recorder and for some reason the sound doesn't reproduce well on our machine. Undeterred, she sings along, wailing with her eyes closed, snapping her fingers in time with the warbling sound of the recorder. She fast-forwards and tries another song. She tells us we don't have to worry when we're away. She was in Vietnam. She knows how to handle herself.

84

Malibu Beach

Hervé, Sandy and I take her around the house and describe our chores. Neither Sandy nor I feels comfortable about her staying in the house when we're gone and before she leaves I tell her, "We're going to be storing our stereo at a friend's, so bring your own music."

We decide to buy a lock for our door. We don't suspect she'd steal anything but we doubt whether she'd take responsibility for her friends.

Sandy and I drive to the airport and meet Anne, who appears tired and nervous. While waiting for her luggage she accidently burns a cigarette hole in the sweater of an elderly woman.

"I'm sorry," Anne says, "really I am."

"Oh dear."

"I'm really sorry," Anne repeats. But she can't suppress a giggle.

"Well I don't think an apology is enough."

"Where the hell are my bags?" Anne says. She crushes the cigarette under her heel. "There's one," she says, jockeying to grab it.

"I don't think an apology is enough."

We grab the rest of Anne's baggage and hurry outside. It's the first time she's been in the United States in more than three years. On the way to Sunland, she comments on the tastelessness of the billboards lining the highway. We take the back way to the house so she can enter on a dirt, country road.

Hervé is not home when we arrive. Maribeth tells us he's learning how to ride English from the horse trainers up the road. She has a walkie talkie and is awaiting word from him. She says he was just told he'll have to ride English on a pony for stock shots in Hawaii.

Sandy, Anne and I walk to the stables where Hervé is taking his lesson. I help him off the horse and he and Anne embrace, Anne saying, "Hi there, Irving Dwarf."

Their embrace has the warmth of the old days. They laugh, hold hands and walk ahead on the way home.

Relaxing after a day's shooting

Home. The word claims my thoughts as we return to the house. We live here, the four of us, the way we dreamed it briefly in '72.

Anne unpacks and gives Hervé a present, a hand-knitted wool sweater with a brilliantly colored design. He loves it.

But our champagne mood fizzes before dinner when Hervé takes to brooding while completing some paper work. He's also cooking two steaks in the oven.

"Is the steak ready?" Anne asks.

"Anne," he snaps, "check it yourself. I'm busy."

The warm glow of our reunion is gone for the evening and we withdraw into ourselves. Sandy and I head upstairs to finish packing.

August 26th

We awaken at 6:00 a.m. and complete last minute details, installing a lock on the door, packing camera equipment, and stashing our stereo in the room. We're thinking of trade winds and guava trees, volcanoes and waterfalls.

Anne and Hervé are downstairs making coffee, throwing clothes into a suitcase and leaving instructions for various people.

At 6:30, Jim Campbell arrives in a chauffeur-driven limousine. A second bodyguard is with him for extra protection at the airport. We leave the house at 7:00, four cups of espresso in hand, and are driven to the L.A. airport; our mood is ebullient.

At the airport we're joined by a third bodyguard but the heavy protection is unneeded. Passers-by merely point and gawk at Hervé, whispering "There's Tattoo from 'Fantasy Island.'"

We're driven through the airport lobby aboard a golf cart, sandwiched between two bodyguards and trailed by Jim

Arriving at Maui Airport

Campbell who trots behind us. After an hour's wait in the private Presidential Club, we board the plane, Anne and Hervé in first class, Sandy and I in coach.

Two hours out of L.A. a stewardess tells us our friends in first class would like us to visit them. We do so and share the flight with them, story-telling, drinking, laughing and catching up on the lost years of our friendship.

We land in Honolulu and take a forty-minute connecting flight to Maui. We're met at the Maui airport by a young woman, a friend of Hervé's. Susie's a transplanted New Yorker.

We drive a rented car to the Sheraton Maui and settle into adjacent rooms whose balconies overlook the brilliantly hued ocean. We have lunch in town and then, exhausted from the trip, return to the Sheraton to rest in our rooms.

That evening we meet Susie's partner, Rick, and share some beer on his fishing boat. Rick offers to take us fishing tomorrow. We agree to meet at 1:00 p.m. The four of us fade fast and return to the Sheraton, enjoying the sweet natural flow of our friendship. Hervé runs ahead and from the second story balcony looks down on us and declares himself "Pope Pedro."

August 27th

At breakfast Hervé rivets the eyes of tourists in the dining room. He refuses to sign any autographs, telling disappointed fans, "Sorry, I'm on vacation." He tells me that he doesn't want any photographs taken of him. Suddenly I feel like a bodyguard.

He wants to kick off his vacation with an exotic drink but the bar doesn't open until eleven. While discussing what to do in the half hour before the bar opens, a young woman

Skimming the South Pacific in "The Shell"

approaches him and says, "I'd like to show you *my* tattoo."

He smiles at her, "Sure, sure."

The woman lifts her pants leg and reveals an ankle with the word "Tattoo" written next to a scarred, almost obliterated, tattoo of a rose. Hervé asks me to take a photograph of her tattoo, with him standing next to her. The bar opens.

Hervé orders a rum drink and asks the woman, "What happened to the rose?"

"I cut it with a knife and it got infected real bad."

We leave the hotel to buy supplies for the fishing expedition: three six-packs of beer, one bottle of wine, bread and cheese. We board "The Shell," a stylish fishing boat with mid-1800's New Orleans look and Maui ambiance. It has parquet floors, a well-equipped galley, highly polished wood steering wheels on deck and below, and cosy below-deck berths.

We meet Susie and Rick and several of their friends. Suntan oil is passed around and soon "The Shell" is skimming over the South Pacific.

We spend the afternoon relaxing, easing L.A. body/mind tension overboard in stages.

Anne and Hervé are still somewhat tentative toward each other but how could they be otherwise? They're divorced and their reconciliation is with an eye toward living together without any restraints on either's freedom. Their present relationship has yet to find its own comfortable rhythms.

We don't catch any fish but no one cares. It's been a perfect day.

August 28th

Mid-morning we drive our rented Malibu toward a highly touted volcano. We head up a snaking road and pause only

A contemplative moment

when Sandy says, "Scott, pull over. I think I see some mushrooms."

Hervé is startled. "Mushrooms? Where?"

Sandy points to a spot about twenty-five yards off the road. She gets out, goes there, and returns five minutes later with a handful of what look like Maui's world-renowned psychotropic mushrooms.

Hervé is incredulous. "How'd you see them? They were so far away."

We continue the drive to the volcano's cloud-shrouded lip. We get out into a misty rain, and stare into the volcano's silent, foggy innards. Hervé walks to another edge and gazes down. When he rejoins us five minutes later, he's in the subdued mood of someone who's been staring into the abyss.

We start back, stopping along the way to pick Maui mushrooms. A bus-load of tourists stops. They've spotted Hervé picking mushrooms.

Someone raises a camera and I step in front of him.

"Please," I say, "no photos. Hervé is on vacation."

The tourist lowers his camera. We return to our car and Hervé examines a map of Maui. He directs me to go to Hana, on the opposite tip of the island.

Anne wants to see where Hana is located but Hervé refuses to give her the map. He's having stomach cramps and his mood tightens with his stomach.

Worried about his health, Anne again asks to see the map. He refuses. Welcome to Bad Time In Hawaii.

We travel in silence with Hervé standing, holding his stomach. Does he want to go back to the Sheraton? No, he wants to go to Hana. It starts to rain as we enter the first of hundreds of hairpin turns. The narrow road runs along a cornice, carved from a cliff. As I drive in the rain Hervé stands behind me, mentally steering us around the treacherous turns. Large oncoming cars several times force us off the road.

He clutches his heart and says, "I ought to race you in

Monte Carlo, the way you're driving. Honk around the corners. That's the way the French do it."

We arrive in Hana at five that afternoon. It's still raining. No restaurants are open so we go into a bar and sit at a table. We order drinks and Sandy and Anne go to the ladies' room. Hervé and I sip our drinks.

He looks up and says, "Why don't we all get one big room and all get laid?"

I sip my drink.

He sips his drink.

I sip my drink.

Anne and Sandy return to the table and Hervé tells them, "I think we should get a hotel room and spend the night in Hana. It's too late to go back tonight. In this rain it's dangerous."

"What about our flight to Kauai tomorrow morning?" Sandy asks.

"It can be postponed," Hervé answers.

"Let's go back tonight," I say. "Our rooms are paid for at the Sheraton."

"It's too dangerous," he counters. "The roads are slippery. You saw how many times you had to drive off the road on the way here."

I shrug. "I don't think it was that dangerous. I'd like to go back tonight. What do you think, Sandy?"

She replies, "It's O.K. with me. You're the one who's driving."

Hervé reluctantly agrees to return to the Sheraton. We finish our drinks and walk through the downpour to our car.

As I steer around the first hairpin turn, a Volkswagon rounds the corner, skids across the road and slams into our Malibu, striking the door next to Hervé. The Malibu caroms onto the shoulder of the road and stops a few feet from the precipice. The Volkswagon skids another twenty feet down the road and stops.

"Everyone O.K.?" I ask.

95

I step out into the rain and walk toward the driver of the Volkswagon who staggers toward me. He's tall, Hawaiian, and very drunk. He's sorry, it was his fault. As we exchange driver's licenses we're joined by a policeman. The Hana police station happens to be close by.

"I saw the accident," the policeman says. Hervé joins us, address book in hand, camera strapped from his neck.

"Then you know it was this man's fault," I tell the policeman.

"Yes, I saw the whole thing."

A young boy runs towards us, paper in one hand, pen in the other. Hervé's worked up a pretty good head of steam by now so I motion to the boy—Please, not now. He stops in his tracks. The policeman affirms my gesture with a glance.

Hervé photographs both cars from several angles before we return to our car.

"Shit," he says as we complete the first turn. "My address book. Look at it. The rain washed away the names on the first pages."

An hour of hairpin turns follows without a word exchanged. Night falls. The rain lets up. Hervé leans over the front seat and, in a Shirley Temple voice, says, "Scotty, can we stop? I have to go pee pee."

We laugh and the tension lifts. We're back at the Sheraton by 11; everyone's too tired to even *have* a mood.

August 29th

We're tourists all morning, strolling up and down the boutique-studded main drag of town. Many passers-by recognize Hervé; some merely point, others come up to tell him

96

how much they love "Fantasy Island." A few ask for autographs and Hervé, friendly but firm, tells them no, this is his vacation.

Our flight to Kauai is postponed to four that afternoon so we drive to a deserted beach for a picnic: champagne, cheese and pickled Mauian onions. Then on to the airport where I fill out an accident report at the car rental. We have drinks in the bar and board the plane to Kauai.

During the short flight, Hervé writes on his air-sickness bag: "Good Health—love Tattoo—Hervé Villechaize." I hand the bag to three very stoned passengers seated nearby. They cackle appreciation and wave thanks.

Kauai Airport. We take a taxi to the Coco Palms Hotel. Kauai is greener, wetter, and hillier than Maui. It sports fishtail ferns, white ginger, plumeria, flowering vines, trees and shrubs, and cascading waterfalls, for starters. Feels great to be here.

The four of us share Kai IV, a suite of rooms decorated in overbright colors. Hervé's and Anne's side of the suite has a king-size bed, small kitchen, dining area and living room. Our adjoining room is smaller but airy and light with the same view: the tops of palm trees, a parking lot, highway, beach and the South Pacific.

Hervé joins a few of his "Fantasy Island" friends and when he returns late that afternoon he's tired but upbeat and considerate. "Use room service," he tells us. "If you want something, just ask for it. Impose yourself." He picks up on our jovial mood. "You didn't eat those mushrooms, did you?"

"We nibbled on a few of them," Anne confesses. "But nothing's happened."

"You're crazy," he tells her. "All of you...they could be poisonous."

We wait all evening for something to happen, but nothing does.

August 30th

Dawn. Hervé leaves for work; "Fantasy Island" is shooting stock shots.

We sleep late and awaken feeling great. We call room service and, with Anne, order breakfast which is wheeled in on silver trays about a half hour later. Omelets, papaya and coffee; we relax into Kauai's sweet aloha. The three of us spend the afternoon exploring the Coconut Grove, the Coco Palms zoo and back roads.

Evening. The four of us take a taxi to a nearby Holiday Inn, where we've been invited to see a troupe of hula dancers perform. The dancers are hula-hot and have Hervé in mind. During one dance, instead of punctuating their hula with cries of "Souee! Souee!" they shout "Tattoo! Tattoo!" They're backed by a rhumba band and a fire eater.

After the show the performers pull up chairs and gush affection for Hervé. They watch him every week on television and are thrilled to be with him. And Hervé doesn't let them down. He's charming.

Someone suggests that we all go to a nearby disco. We shift locations en masse and step onto the dance floor, laughing, enjoying the high-spirited evening.

August 31st

Sunrise. The four of us are driven in a trailer past farmlands and small towns with the South Pacific below and to our left. We drive for forty minutes to what our Hawaiian driver describes as "the Allerton estate. About six hundred unspoiled acres, the *old* Hawaii." He fills us in on the Allerton legend. "He's considered the Howard Hughes of Hawaii. He's been living here maybe sixty years. Not many people have ever seen the place. We're lucky to see it."

We drive onto the estate after passing inspection at the guarded front gate. Our driver tells us that Allerton's father made twenty to thirty million while still in his twenties. "He made it in the stockyards in Chicago from 1910 to 1920. Then Allerton Sr. and his brother packed up and moved to Hawaii. And they bought this part of Kauai."

I ask the driver, "Why is he allowing 'Fantasy Island' to film stock shots of his Shangrila?"

"Who knows. He just decided."

We park alongside other trailers and Hervé steps out to the immediate attention of a hairdresser, a make-up artist, and a wardrobe assistant.

Sandy and I stroll along the manicured expanse of lawn in front of Mr. Allerton's elegant house. We pass beneath coconut trees and find the hula dancers and the fire eater from the night before; they're extras for "Fantasy Island" today, sweet, beautiful and bubbly as champagne. We hang out with them for a while and then explore jungle pathways behind the house. We return for a luncheon buffet with the crew and cast.

Camera around my neck, I'm singled out by Nora, the make-up artist. "Excuse me," she says. "Could I ask a favor?"

"Sure."

"Well, Ricardo looks so handsome in his white riding suit, I'd love to have a picture of me with him."

Before I can answer she turns to Ricardo Montalban and says, "Come, Ricardo." She takes his arm. "One picture. I was just commenting on how handsome you look today."

Do I have any shots left in my camera? I check and I'm

on 36. Or maybe I've taken 36. I frame them. Ricardo is hungry but patient. "Make sure you take your light reading from the foreground," he says. They have their arms around each other. Ricardo breaks into a broad smile which he quickly reduces to 35mm proportions. I snap what turns out to be my last shot.

We return to the buffet and fill paper plates with macaroni, cheese, shrimp, meat and chocolate mousse. I sit down next to Ricardo at a long, crowded table.

Ricardo is talking with a cameraman about some aspects of modern life. He talks passionately about the lack of societal morality and the loss of values in general. "Honor and modesty are two values gone from current life," he says.

After lunch, Hervé and Ricardo are filmed in a Rover, up and down a dirt road, perhaps a dozen times. It's the type of "acting" for which Hervé has little patience. That evening the four of us have dinner together in a seafood restaurant and Hervé's mood is unexplainably black hole. We dine around his mood.

September 1st

Hervé's depressed moods are all-enveloping. When he returns from work around seven he grunts hello to us. We meet him later in the Coco Palms bar and are quickly silenced by His Mood. By the time we leave the bar to go to a party, I feel like returning to our room. You can't leave, I tell myself. You're the bodyguard.

We walk to a hotel where a buffet dinner party for the crew is in half swing. When Hervé enters, there's a rush of attention toward him. People joke with him and fawn over

Ricardo Montalban and Hervé Villechaize on Kauai

At full gallop

Out riding, Hervé meets "Fantasy Island" extras

Shooting "Fantasy Island" stock shots

Racing on the beach

him. He circulates, charming, laughing, shaking hands, giving them their ultimate fix.

The hula dancers arrive and we go next door with them to a disco.

But Sandy and I don't feel much like dancing. We watch Hervé with the hula dancers, radiant, his warmth going out to them. And I recall what Anne said, the morning after we met the hula dancers. "When you're with them, you're the life of the party. But after, pfft, there's nothing left for me. You go to sleep."

September 2nd

Hervé rents a car and I drive through the fertile countryside of Kauai. Later, we stop at a small grocery store and ask directions to a local restaurant. The young man we ask is in the driver's seat of a mud-covered, rusted, barely alive sixties stationwagon. He gets so excited that he hops out of his car, jumps up and down and says, "I'll take you to Alfredo's myself! Just a second!" He runs into the store, shouting, "Mammy! Mammy! Come quick! It's that little guy from 'Fantasy Island.'"

Mammy is unrushed. She eases herself from the store to their car. We follow the mud-covered noise to Alfredo's Restaurant.

There, the young man introduces himself. "My name is Melville Lee Dickens. Some say I'm related to the author, Charles Dickens."

Hervé steps to one side with me and quietly asks, "You want to invite them for a drink?"

"Sure."

Melville can't believe his ears. "You *bet* we want to have

a drink with you." He rushes to his car, returning with Mammy and an Instamatic camera. Beaming, he says, "This here is my wife, Mammy."

We introduce ourselves. Melville snaps a picture of Mammy and Hervé and the six of us walk into Alfredo's.

Melville, in unasked explanation of his sing-song speech says, "I was in a car accident. Dragged ninety-five feet. Opened my head like an eggshell." He parts his dirty hair with his hands and shows us the scars. Then he displays another scar on a knuckle. "Cut it to the bone with a chainsaw one day." He says he's been living in the stationwagon with Mammy for the last two years.

"You want something to eat?" Hervé asks.

Melville shrugs, shyly, slightly embarrassed. He looks at the menu in front of him. "Well, yeah, sure, thanks."

We order sandwiches and Melville confides, "I have a son by my first wife. I once took poison and a bottle of Anacin when they took my little boy away from me." He gestures toward Mammy. "My second wife. Married five years now but I have no child from this wife." He returns to his story about the poison. "I didn't die from it, though, because the Anacin coated my stomach."

"How do you live?" Hervé asks.

"Disability," Melville replies. "Also, Mammy makes shell necklaces. Go get one of your necklaces, honey," he suggests.

"It isn't finished," she tells him.

Hervé assures her, "It doesn't matter. I'd like to see it as it is."

Mammy smiles tentatively, then leaves the table. She returns ten minutes later with a finished necklace which she gives to Hervé. He admires it and kisses Mammy on both cheeks. "I love it," he tells her. Mammy laughs softly and Hervé wears the necklace wrapped around his wrist.

Before leaving, Hervé asks Melville, "How would you really like to earn a living?"

Melville pauses and says, "I could be a driver."

107

"Give me your name and address. I know some drivers on the island. I'll ask about a job for you."

Melville claps his hands. "Oh boy!" He writes on a scrap of paper and hands it to Hervé. "It's my father's name and address and phone number. He'll know where to find me when he finds out who's calling me."

We part company. We drive to the northern tip of the island and climb to a lookout point. The valley below us is emerald green; the distant mountains look Peruvian. As we watch the sun set, three hunters appear carrying rifles.

"What are you hunting?" Hervé calls out.

"Wild goats."

"How do you get the goats after you shoot them?"

"I see 'em. There are trails leading down."

"Let's get out of here," I suggest. I *am* the bodyguard.

September 3rd

We have an early breakfast and meet Andy, our driver and companion for the day. He's Hawaiian, friendly, and eager to show us his island. We buy supplies for the day: a styrofoam cooler, two six-packs of beer, cheese, wine and poy (a starchy bean paste).

Andy maneuvers the four-wheel-drive Rover through the countryside, past deep canyons and broad valleys, through sugar cane fields and onto a rocky, secluded road. We park when we can go no farther, gather our camera gear, remove our shoes and socks and follow Andy along the path. We pick and eat sweet guavas and are led to what Andy calls "The Slippery Slide." It's an idyllic spot. Surrounded by dense jungle, a slow-moving stream spills over a sloping sheet of rock and drops thirty feet into a pool of water.

Andy, in swim trunks, demonstrates. He shoots down The

In the shallow lagoon

Slippery Slide on his belly and splashes head first into the pool. Surfacing, he waves for us to follow him down. We hesitate.

"Try it, it's fun," he calls.

Hervé has other ideas. He wants to shoot some Super 8 while walking in the shallow lagoon that empties over The Slippery Slide. Andy gives him a life preserver. Hervé steps into the water, buoyed by the preserver, and glides along, walking on tiptoes. He's inspired by the beauty and risk of the moment and films with the camera a few inches above the gently flowing water.

Several strangers arrive and gawk at Hervé. Paradise lost—momentarily.

We return to the Rover and Andy drives us to a spectacular waterfall, hidden from the road. It's now raining.

We walk toward the falls and, with no one in sight, Hervé impulsively hands me his camera and takes off his swim suit. Standing naked in front of us he says, "Shoot a roll of me under the falls. This is too much!"

I tell him the camera lens is streaked with water.

"It doesn't matter," he calls back. "It'll be more realistic with the water on the lens. I like things au naturel." He walks on the wet rocks leading to the crashing falls and climbs the slippery embankment with the surefootedness of a mountain goat. He stands under the falls, then bows, hands in prayer. He prostrates himself. I shoot the roll. He returns, exhilarated.

"Fantastic," he says. "What film is in your camera?"

"Fuji."

"Good. Take some stills of me under the falls." He is glistening naked. "A position to shoot from would be up there." He points to a rocky ledge on the crest of a hill. Then he climbs up the watersmooth rocks to the falls and I climb up the hill to the rocky ledge.

Again he communes with the falls, "like an American Indian" he will later say. I photograph him as he performs the same reverential gestures.

Shooting Super 8 at "The Slippery Slide"

Homage to nature under the waterfall

Communing

"Incredible," he exults as we all head for the Rover. "Incredible." He replaces his camera in its case. "This is what makes me happy."

We drive to the northern coast of Kauai, and park on a road overlooking the beach and the Pacific Ocean.

Andy says, "I've got to go visit a horse." He points to a tree.

Hervé laughs. "I've got to visit the same horse."

"Think I'll do the same," I add.

It's late afternoon; the sun barely dominates the sky. Sandy and Anne walk to the beach and lie down near the water's edge. The three of us soon join them. Everyone's in a mellow mood.

We relax for a half hour and are about to leave when Hervé suddenly darts toward the water.

"Be careful," we call after him.

He laughs, oblivious to the moss-covered rocks in the water. Splashing, he slips, is upended, and lands on his head.

We race to him and Andy picks him up. He carries and sets Hervé down gently on the soft earth near the Rover. Gasping to consciousness, Hervé tries to stand up and walk but loses his balance. We catch him. He breaks our support and swings his fists wildly. He spins and falls. We help him up and into the back seat of the Rover. He sits between Sandy and Anne and holds his head in his hands.

I sit with Andy who speeds toward Wilcox Hospital, about an hour away.

Hervé's face is gray, his eyes are half closed. His head rests on a towel. He moans, "What happened?"

Anne tells him, "You fell and hit your head."

"Did I pass out?"

"Yes."

"For how long?"

"A few minutes."

"Did I pass out?"

"Yes."

"How long?"

"A few minutes. How do you feel?"

"I'm dizzy. I passed out?"

"Yes."

"How long?"

"Only a few minutes."

"I did?"

"Yes."

He grimaces, closes his eyes, falls asleep, awakens a few minutes later. Moaning, he holds the back of his head with his hands. "Oooooh. What happened?"

Sandy tells him, "You fell on a rock and hit your head."

"Did I pass out? I don't remember."

"Yes, you passed out."

"How long?"

"A few minutes."

"I did?"

"Yes."

He dozes again.

I'm dropped off at the Coco Palms so I can drive the rented car to the hospital.

Hervé is helped into Emergency at Wilcox Hospital. He signs in, "Hervé Villechaize. No sex!"

He's taken to a private room on the fourth floor. It's 8:00 p.m. and he says his head is still ringing with pain.

September 4th

After an early breakfast, we drive to the hospital. Hervé is dispirited, dizzy, still in pain, and restless. He wants to return to the Coco Palms but his doctor wants to keep him another day for observation. He's suffered a concussion. He

115

tells us that a nurse awakened him at 4:00 a.m. and asked for three inscribed autographs.

"Did you?" I ask.

"Sure. You don't fool around when they've got your life in their hands."

The three of us leave around noon so he can sleep.

We return to the hospital at six and find him in better spirits. He's been visited throughout the day by hula dancers, and his doctor says he'll be discharged tomorrow morning. We visit with him until eight and then go to dinner. Andy is in the restaurant, blind drunk, waving for us to join him and his friends at their table. We have a drink with him. He insists it was his fault. We assure him the accident was just that—an accident.

September 5th

Hervé is feeling better though he's still dizzy when he turns his head to the left or right. He checks out of the hospital, holding Anne's and Sandy's hands for support. We stop at a record shop and the store owner asks him, "How you feeling? I heard on the radio you had an accident." Hervé says he's doing all right. He buys several Hawaiian cassette tapes and suddenly he's shopping for fabric.

We pick up a copy of *The Honolulu Advertiser* and read about his accident. "The inside, exclusive super-doop scoop today is that Hervé Villechaize, the midget who stars on TV's 'Fantasy Island' (and was so great in the movie, 'The One and Only'), was emergency-rushed to Wilcox Memorial Hospital on Kauai Sunday. The 3 foot 10 member of the 'Fantasy Island' cast and crew finished filming Saturday, slipped on a rock while running along the beach and suffered a concussion. The good news: When we spoke with him

116

last night he was in good spirits—and he expects to be released from the hospital today."

Hervé calls his agent, Arnold Rifkin, and his producer, Michael Fisher about the accident. They urge him to recuperate before flying back to Los Angeles.

That night an angelic Hawaiian girl, maybe ten years old, approaches our table and offers a gift to Hervé—a map of Kauai and a half dozen ball point pens. Hervé is touched by the gift. He receives it as gently as it was given.

September 6th

We exchange our rented Malibu for a sun-yellow, Volks-wagon convertible and drive to Princeville. I shift gears with the care of an egg handler; Hervé's head still throbs with pain and he's dizzy from time to time. I ease over bumps in the road. The sun is beating down on us so I suggest that he buy a hat in Princeville. We try several stores but he doesn't find a hat he likes. We all urge that he buy *any* hat for protection from the sun. He ignores the suggestion.

September 7th

We spend the day touring the island in our convertible. Hervé stands up in the back seat, taking in the Hawaiian countryside through dark sunglasses.

We shop for shells and fabric and everywhere we go people ask him how he's feeling.

We're rescheduled to fly back to L.A. tomorrow evening.

117

Hervé suggests we have a farewell party in Kai IV. Sounds like a great idea. We invite the hula dancers, the fire eater, and a few of Kauai's more off-beat beats.

I remind myself that I'm the bodyguard. It occurs to me that one of the hula dancers is fifteen years old and there will be a couple of seven-or eight-year-olds at the party. I figure that several of those invited will light up joints as naturally as they smile hello when they see you.

I suggest to Hervé that maybe we should ask the tokers to toke-up before coming to the party.

"Why?"

"Because there will be several underage people at the party and it might be better if you didn't risk another newspaper story."

His eyes blaze. "People can do whatever they want. If they want to smoke—let them smoke. I'm not going to start telling people what they can or can't do."

"It was only a suggestion. Do what you want."

He crosses his hands on his chest and fumes, "I'm tired of hanging out with straight people. They bore me. When we get back that's finished."

We fall silent.

That night, after the party, we end up at Buzz's, an aptly named restaurant. The joint is jumping with hip scenes within scenes played out in bamboo cubicles around tables, like so many hands of a poker game.

Everyone has seized on the birthday of the restaurant owner to celebrate. The place is packed, smoky, and swinging to the music of a guitarist and drummer who set the stage for a belly dancer.

The belly dancer undulates affectionately around the instruments and cubicles of cheering friends. There's an abundance of goodwill in the room and it's infectious.

September 8th

Andy describes Mennehunie Pond. We ask what it is and he tells us about the legendary Mennehunies: "Very small people. Two feet high. Said to live in a tropical forest surrounding what's called the Mennehunie Pond."

I drive everyone to the Mennehunie Pond and tell Hervé, "This is like your 'Roots.' You're going home at last."

He laughs. "That's what I'll call my ranch in Los Angeles— 'The Mennehunie Ranch.'"

We return to the hotel, check out, and transfer our luggage to the taxi-van belonging to Steve (the fire eater). Steve drives us and several hula dancers to the airport. Other hula dancers, Andy, and still others from the previous night's party are there. The hula dancers give us farewell ginger leis, hugs and kisses.

It's early evening. As the plane taxis down the runway we signal to our Kauai friends with pen lights. They signal back with lit candles.

Jim Campbell and Maribeth meet us at the L.A. airport. We claim our luggage and get into a black limousine. Hervé says his head still hurts and he's still dizzy.

Jim and Maribeth tail the limo back to Hervé's house. Sandy and I feel the need for some time alone. Hervé and Anne apparently feel the same need.

Later, I find Hervé near the pool, furious, picking up the remains of a barbeque party: greasy paper plates, cups, charred bones, wine bottles.

"Look at the place," he says angrily. "She left it a mess. The plants are half-dead."

Sandy and I clear and clean. I rake the leaves.

He suddenly turns toward me. "Remember that time, at

Jim and Rene's? We all had a picnic at their country place, remember?"

"Yes, I remember."

"You said you'd cut their lawn with your teeth to be able to live there."

"I was joking."

"Well," he points to the lawn, "you can start cutting."

"I said I was joking."

He stalks into the house, leaving the screen door open. I continue to rake. When I finish, I return to the house and close the screen door. Dozens of flies now do figure-eights inside. Hervé is in the kitchen. When he goes out, he leaves the screen door wide open again. I close it. Several more times he leaves the door open and I close it.

Finally I ask him, "Hey, Hervé, when you go out, would you mind closing the screen door behind you? Flies keep coming in."

"I like flies," he replies. "This is the country. The flies remind me that I'm in the country."

Sandy and I retreat upstairs, subdued by Hervé's chilly attitude toward us.

The following morning I stare at the kitchen blackboard. Hervé has divided the chores to be done around the house that day into two sections: Anne, and S&S. Anne's chores: make marmalade, sew Hawaiian fabric around pillows. Written under our initials: water plants, feed cats, chop wood. Sandy and I have been doing these chores unasked since the day we arrived. I'm put off by the listing on the blackboard. Something about it smacks of plantation days.

The following morning the same chores are freshly written under our initials. I erase our chores from the blackboard.

The chillyness now extends to our relationship with Anne who is distant and non-communicative.

Nothing seems to be working out. Dena, (the house-sitter who left the place in a shambles) stops by for her house-sitting money. As Hervé relates the story, "I asked her how much? She said, 'You decide.' I said, 'No, just tell me.' So

120

she said, 'O.K.—two hundred and fifty dollars.' Unbelievable! I had to give her the money."

I ask, "Why didn't you tell her it was too much?"

His hands clench. "I don't like to talk about money."

The freeze continues. We're persona non grata. Our communication is reduced to chores written and erased on the kitchen blackboard. I continue to do chores but I no longer chop wood. I don't feel much like working on Maggie's farm no more.

A few days later, a still photographer shows up with Hervé's public relations agent. The agent has hired the photographer to shoot stills of Hervé on the ranch.

When I see Hervé I remind him, "Before we went to Hawaii you said I had a job when we returned, shooting stock shots of you around the ranch."

He shakes his head. "I said there was a *possibility* of a job. It was up to you to act on it. You didn't act so they hired someone else."

I've seen this movie before.

The freeze-out thaws the same day Hervé fires Miguel, who's been building a rabbit hutch. Miguel worked five hours the previous Saturday and not the eleven for which he charged. Hervé fires him when he discovers this.

Miguel shrugs. "I can get work with someone else for $7.00 an hour."

"Fine," Hervé tells him. "Work elsewhere."

He tells several of the neighborhood girls that Miguel was fired and there's still work to do on the rabbit hutch. The girls offer to help. He talks with us about the generosity of their offer.

I enter the spirit of the thaw and tell him, "Let's finish the job on Saturday. We'll get some beer and Coca-Cola and we'll all get into it."

He agrees, and that night we're our old selves for the first time since Hawaii. Sandy gives him a present from the three of us, a book about the Mennehunies.

I spend Saturday building the hutch with Anne and Hervé.

During the day, Hervé's public relations agent phones and tells him he's going to be on "The Merv Griffin Show" on Monday. Hervé asks me, "Do you have your Hawaiian slides back yet?"

"No, not yet. I called on Friday. They'll be in on Monday."

"No good. They have to know about the slides tonight."

"I'll get them Monday morning. If they're not in I'll get them from Kodak."

He shakes his head. "Too many ifs. I've got to know for sure today. I have to think of a format for the show. I have to do that before Monday."

Early Monday morning, I hear Hervé making espresso downstairs. I put on a robe and join him. "Have you thought of a format for the show yet?"

"No, not yet."

"If my slides are ready I'll bring them to you on the set." He's receptive to the idea now that it's almost show time.

"I'll leave a pass for you."

At 9:30 I call the photo lab and ask if my slides have come in. They haven't.

"Can I get them from Kodak directly?"

"Well," the voice on the phone says, "Kodak is in Palo Alto."

"Is that far?"

"North of San Francisco."

"Too far."

Without the slides, Hervé talks on "The Merv Griffin Show" about his trip to Hawaii.

The following day chores reappear for us on the blackboard. The blackboard again becomes Hervé's only form of communication. I start one of the chores, "Move cinderblocks to rabbit hutch," but pull my back unloading the wheelbarrow, and quit.

A few days later, Hervé tells Sandy he wants to speak to me.

When I see him I say, "You want to talk to me?"

"After you finish your breakfast."

"O.K.," I say when I'm finished, "let's talk."

He looks at Anne and Sandy. "Let's go outside. It's too hot in here."

We follow him out.

He begins by asking for the color photographs I took of him. He examines them. Some were taken before Hawaii at Malibu beach and show him fishing.

"I like these," he says. "But you should have taken a few close-ups. You need close-ups if you want to sell them."

"After a day's work I thought you might not want someone clicking away at you with a camera."

"I don't mind. People do it all the time." He looks closely at the photos and tells me the finish is too grainy.

"I asked for semi-gloss."

"Did you ask for the white borders?"

"No. I told the guy *no* border. I told him two things. Semi-gloss and no border."

"Do you have the bill?"

I get it. He looks at it. "$42.00? Send them back. You want to send them back?"

"Yeah."

"O.K., I'll call them and they'll return your money." He telephones the photo lab and the Villechaize name brings the desired result. "Return the photos and you'll get your money back."

He pauses. "Now, what I wanted to talk to you about. Lately almost no work has been done around the house. I leave messages for things to be done and they're not done. Since we got back from Hawaii you haven't done any work. We decided we would each work three hours every day."

"Hervé," I say, "we never decided anything. You mentioned it and we agreed to talk about it after Hawaii. Remember?"

"All I know is that since Hawaii you haven't done any work around here."

123

"That's right. And since Hawaii you've excluded us from your life. You've reduced our relationship to messages on a blackboard."

"I have no time! What am I supposed to do?"

"Talk to us," Sandy suggests. "You don't even say 'Hello' anymore when you come home from work."

Anne takes in the unfolding argument without entering it.

Hervé says sharply, "I'm going to have to tighten the reins."

The phrase "tighten the reins" gets to me. "What are you talking about?"

"I ask you to move a pile of cinderblocks to the rabbit hutch. When I come back from work you've moved ten cinderblocks."

"I wrenched my back."

"You hurt your back moving ten cinderblocks?"

"That's right."

"You couldn't have. Not ten cinderblocks. I carry them myself."

"If you have a bad back it can go from *one* cinderblock."

He frowns. "How are you going to help build the studio with a bad back? What good will you be to me? There's a lot of work to be done around here."

I'm stung by his words, "What good will you be to me." I turn, walk to the road, and continue walking for about a half mile. An hour passes. When I return, Hervé is conciliatory.

"I talked with Sandy. I didn't know you both felt that way. I understand now. I let things go on for too long. A mistake. It won't happen again."

For the first time in our relationship I don't quite believe him. I talk later with Sandy. She fills me in on the hot discussion that continued after I left, which culminated in her telling Hervé, "All you're interested in now is how much work Scott can do for you around here. You're a phony."

"You told him what?"

"That he's a phony."

"What did he say?"

"He said, 'I'm not a phony. You better not say that again. I won't stand for anybody insulting me in my house.'"

"And?"

"Then I started to cry. I told him, 'I don't want to hurt you. But you're driving us away. We didn't come out here to be farmhands. Scott has to spend more time on his writing.'"

"What did he say?"

"He said he understood our feelings about being excluded. He said we'll have to have discussions so tension doesn't build up again. We hugged and that's how it ended."

"I've got to talk with him."

I find him at the stables leaning pensively against a railing. He tells me, "From now on we'll have a meeting once a week to discuss things. I'll find the time."

Later, he tells all of us, "I'll order a bottle of four hundred valium so we'll have them for bad moments like this."

For a few days we make a concerted effort to rekindle our eight-year friendship. But the spontaneity is gone, replaced by wariness. At most, we trade superficialities. I send out a peace feeler.

"I'd like to talk abut the four of us."

Hervé tenses. "I don't have time to talk."

"Why did you turn on us after Hawaii?"

He says nothing for a moment. "Just little things."

"Like what?"

"Like taking me for granted."

He refuses to give specifics. Then he says, bitterly, "Once an insult is said it can't be withdrawn." He refers to Sandy's calling him a phony. "What was said that morning can't be erased. The power of words is like that."

The following night, Hervé and Anne return to the house with Maribeth. They're in good spirits. Hervé shows us an article about him in *The National Enquirer* and a take-off in *Mad Magazine* on "Fantasy Island."

When I'm alone with him later that night his cheerful mood changes suddenly to anger. He paces and says, "I woke up at three in the morning and decided I don't have to take this shit. Today I had two shows and I didn't know my lines. I kept thinking, I don't have to be in a good mood when I come home. I don't have to say 'Hello' and all that bullshit."

"Nobody's asking you to be in a good mood. All we're asking is for you to recognize the existence of the people you're living with—the people who really care about you."

"I've had enough of this. I didn't let the two girls stay in the house because of you."

"The runaways?"

"Yes. Both of you were so uptight I had to tell them not to come."

"They're thirteen and fifteen. The cops had been here and we thought we were being set up. Remember? You'd have been crazy to have them live here. Jim Campbell said the same thing. So did Arnold."

"I don't care what they said. I didn't let them stay here because of you and Sandy."

We argue back and forth and suddenly the inevitable dawns on me. "We'll be out of here in a few days."

He's taken aback. "When I come home from work I don't want to feel I *have* to say hello to anyone. So I'm asking you to leave my house. I want you out."

"Hervé, I just said we'll be out of here in a few days. Why ask us to leave? We're leaving. Did you say that so you can tell your friends, 'I asked them to leave my house'? Sure sounds better than 'They left.'"

"I want you out of my house."

"Well, now you have what you want. Anne is here. You finally got her back so you don't need us anymore."

"I don't know whether to laugh or cry," he says, shaking his head. "Anne is back."

We look at each other, the loss of our friendship bridging the distance between us. "You know," I say, "it's as if two other people are arguing. It doesn't sound like us."

His face softens and he walks over to me. "You're right. We shouldn't end it like this." He pours cognac into two

126

glasses and hands one to me. "There are opportunities for you in L.A."

"Hervé, so far we've spent five thousand dollars. We're running low. You know that."

We talk until two in the morning. Before we say goodnight, he confides, "There are three Hervés. One is the public Hervé, the TV star 'Tattoo.' Another is the Hervé my friends know. No one knows the third Hervé. That's the one that keeps me alive. It's a candle burning inside me. No one has a chance to blow it out."

Sandy and I decide to return to New York. We arrange with the Sunland Moving Company to pick up our stuff. We want everything stored until we find a place to live in Manhattan.

"Fantasy Island" is shooting in Malibu and Hervé and Anne are away for several days. We pack and watch the World Series.

They return on Thursday evening. On Friday morning Hervé leaves a message on the blackboard before going to work. It reads:

To   ?

There are garbage bags for the compressor not
for the birds—also, empty bottles and cans go,
as you all know, in the garbage. Every morning I
have to do it. *I have no time.*
Keep your newspapers out of my sight.
Signed—the fucking midget

We read the message several times. When Anne comes in we show her the message. She shakes her head. "Boy, that's really rubbing salt in the wound."

"But why?" I ask. "We're leaving. He knows that. Why does he have to end it this way?"

Anne shrugs. "I don't know. That's the way he is. He's always been that way."

"Cruel?"

127

"He can be cruel."

"With his close friends?"

"He drives people away when they get too close to him."

"You're next, Anne. After we're gone he'll need a new scapegoat. First, the bodyguards. Then Miguel. Now us. You're next."

"Oh no," she insists, "if he pulls any of that with me I'm leaving. Pfft. Back to Paris."

On the day of departure, to avoid a final scene we stay in our room until an hour before the movers come. Then we carry forty loaded cartons outside. The moving van backs into the driveway and the move gets under way.

Sandy reenters the house for a forgotten salad bowl and when she returns she tells me she's just seen a surprised Maribeth in the kitchen holding what looked like Hervé's .38 Special. Our pace quickens.

When Hervé leaves the house, he passes Sandy and me without a glance or word.

Maribeth hugs us warmly with eyes filled. "Take care," she says. Sandy tells her, "You take care too. Don't let him do to you what he did to us."

Anne emerges from the house, embraces Sandy and me, and whispers in my ear, "I'll keep in touch."

Hervé's entourage leaves for the Burbank Studios and minutes later we're heading to New York in our packed-to-the-roof Chrysler, on the road again.